Design and Launch an Online

Gift
Business

in a WEEK

Entrepreneur MAGAZINE'S
CLICKSTARTS

Design and Launch an Online
Gift
Business
in a WEEK

◆ *Immediate Profitability with Minimum Startup Investment*

◆ *Unique Business Ideas*

◆ *Programming and Design Knowledge Not Required*

Entrepreneur Press & Cheryl Kimball

Ep
Entrepreneur.
Press

Jere L. Calmes, Publisher
Cover Design: Desktop Miracles
Production and Composition: Eliot House Productions

This publication is designed to provide accurate and authoritative information in regard to the subject matter covered. It is sold with the understanding that the publisher is not engaged in rendering legal, accounting, or other professional services. If legal advice or other expert assistance is required, the services of a competent professional person should be sought.

Computer icon ©Skocko

Hand icon ©newyear2008

Library of Congress Cataloging-in-Publication Data is available
  Kimball, Cheryl.
      Click start: design and launch an online networking business in a week/by Julien A. Sharp.
          p.   cm.   —(Click start series)
        ISBN-13: 978-1-59918-264-3 (alk. paper)
        ISBN-10: 1-59918-264-5 (alk. paper)
            1. Gift shops. 2. Internet marketing. 3. Electronic commerce. 4. New business enter-prises—Management. I. Entrepreneur Media, Inc. II. Title.
      HF5469.6.K56 2009
      658.8'72—dc22   2009000359

Printed in Canada

13 12 11 10 09   10 9 8 7 6 5 4 3 2 1

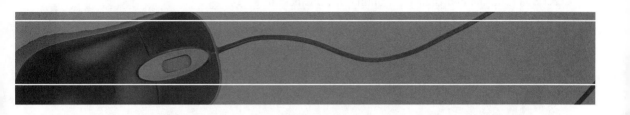

Contents

Chapter 2

Day 1: Thinking Through the Details _ _ _ _ _ _ _ _ _ _ _ _ _ _ _ _ _ 21

Chapter 3

Day 2: Focus on Inventory _ 41

Chapter 7

Day 6: The Merchant Details _____ 127

Chapter 8

Day 7: Online Customer Service _____ 137

Chapter 9

After Day 7: The Tidbits—Growing Your Business, Homebased Issues, and Burnout Prevention _____ 155

Appendix

Resources _____ 169

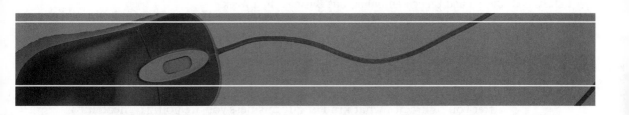

Preface

*T*he internet, the proliferation of online selling, and the willingness of consumers to buy online has changed the small business world as we have known it. Almost anyone can be a part of this exciting business approach—and that includes you. If you have been thinking about having your own business, an online gift business might be just the thing.

The gift business combines fun and business. You can spin off a hobby you love. Or you can come up with something completely different that you think you might like to explore.

After you figure out what kind of gift business you are going to head into, you need to start the hard and important work of figuring out where you are going to find your potential customers. Everything else is important, but this will be the most important work of all. Just as you concentrate on your location and then drive traffic to your brick-and-mortar store, so, too, you do the same with your internet business.

Starting a business of any kind these days is almost synonymous with having an online business. You need to have an online presence no matter what you are selling. This book will help you build this presence both quickly and effectively.

Chapter 1

Before Day 1: Your Gift Business— The Big Picture

*A*lthough online selling is different in many ways from brick-and-mortar selling, starting a business is starting a business no matter what the ultimate sales outlet. So the first thing you need to do before making any specific business decisions is look at the big picture of owning and running a business. This is the general thinking and researching that any business owner must do before taking the plunge. There's no point in even getting to the specifics if you don't consider the big picture first.

Business Ownership

Business ownership is not for everyone. If you lose sleep at night over the smallest of things, you probably aren't a candidate for owning your own business. It can drown you even when things are working out just fine. Some other characteristics of successful business ownership include

- → *the ability to delegate.* Good business owners know that they can't do everything themselves. They also tend to be a tad controlling and want everything done their way, which makes it hard to delegate. Learn how to be a person who lets people do your thing, their way. As long as the end result is what you want, what does it matter how it got there?
- → *organizational skills.* Being disorganized can be the fastest route to disaster. Keep things in order and create a system where you can find things. Keep up with bookkeeping and accounting so that you can make financial decisions at any given moment. Good organization allows you to maintain a high level of inventory control, which is only good for the bottom line.
- → *people skills.* Business owners need many layers of people skills. Needless to say, if you have employees, your people skills need to be topnotch or you need to hire someone whose ability to manage employees is above

---

CLICK TIP

If you do not have a relatively up-to-date desktop computer, you should plan to get one that you dedicate to your online gift business. It should have as much long-term memory as you can afford. Get one with a large-screen monitor and an ergnomic keyboard. Likewise, trick out your office with an ergonomic desktop and chair, and great lighting. Have plenty of open desk space to spread out on to do comparison research. You will spend a lot of time at this computer, so make your work space extremely comfortable!

---

average. But beyond employees, you need to deal with customers, suppliers, shippers, landlords—all people! Learn how to be diplomatic while getting what you want. Also learn to view the other perspective so you can always understand what the real issue is and have a jump on solving it.

Business Planning

Every business needs a plan. Once you decide you want to go into business for yourself, be prepared to put together a plan that outlines almost every detail of your business. Include startup information, personal information about what makes you a good person for this kind of business, financial information including projections about the future income of the business, as well as procedural details. Also look at where your business will be in one, two, three, five, and ten years, letting anyone reading it (including yourself!) realize that you are in control of all aspects of your business.

Creating a Business Plan

You may think that since you plan to start a relatively low-key online business you don't need to take the time and effort required to create a business plan. And you would be wrong. A business plan provides you with many advantages:

- It is a great way to think through the details of your business.
- It is almost a must if you plan to get any outside funding, now or in the future.
- It provides a road map for your business that you can look back on when you feel things are getting a little lost.
- It is a great guide for expanding your business down the road.

Books and websites with sample business plans abound, and you should look at a few before you dig into your own. Don't be intimidated, and think you can't pull this together. If you aren't "a writer," find a friend or freelance writer who can help you. If you aren't "good at math," look for an accountant who will help you pull together the appropriate financials. It is definitely worth it.

Besides books and websites with general information, there are also many business plan templates available to make it easy to plug in your information. The templates will guide you to cover the areas that are expected in a business plan. Also, look to resources like the Small Business Administration and the retired executive program, SCORE. They have lots of useful information on this important part of your business's development.

Whatever route you take, consider the business plan your key to understanding every nook and cranny of your business. The following outlines the main topics your business plan should cover. Also take a look at the Business Plan Checklist on page 17.

An Overview

A business plan should start with a general overview of the business you plan to start. Talk about the online gift business you envision and why you chose this business type. Talk about the niche you plan to fill. The overview should provide enough information for the rest of the business plan to make sense.

Business Logistics

So your main logistical decision is that you are opening an online gift business. Is this an offshoot of a brick-and-mortar storefront? Or strictly online? Outline this information and comment on your choices in this section. Explain your decisions and why you think this is going to work based on what you know about the gift business climate.

Market and Marketing

You need to explain how you determined there is a market for a gift business in the category you have decided to get into. What were the factors that lead you to determine that there is room for another online gift business? What customer type do you plan to target and how do you know they spend money on the gift line you have chosen? That's all your market.

As for marketing, this is where you tell how you are going to let those potential customers know you exist. And when you announce yourself to them, how are you going to entice them to buy from your gift website? This is where you talk about how the online gift industry tends to operate—will you use e-newsletters, coupons, ads in specialty publications?

You

Spend a couple paragraphs talking about your background. How have you prepared to become an entrepreneur? What will make you good at running an online business? And specifically an online gift business?

If you plan to have partners, what are their credentials? And what exactly will they do within the business?

If you plan to hire employees early on, tell whom those employees will be (e.g., a web page manager and a warehouse person) and what they will do to help bring in business.

Business Structure

This brief section covers what kind of business structure you have chosen for your business—a sole proprietorship where you and the business are essentially one and the same thing and the business's income is reported to the IRS as personal income? Or a type of corporation with a separate identity? Or a partnership? And talk briefly about if/how/when that might change in the future.

The Numbers

Numbers need to be crunched even before you take your first order! You want to do monthly revenue projections for the first year of business. How do you plan for your marketing efforts to result in sales?

Be sure to keep tabs on any expenses you incur before you even start taking orders. These startup expenses will be represented differently from your operating expenses.

Another spreadsheet you need is a detailed breakdown of one year of expenses—advertising expenses, employee salaries if applicable, cost of website updating, cost of shipping materials and shipping itself, etc. And then you need to do a balance sheet in which you deduct the expenses from the revenue for each month for a one-year period to see where you stand.

How much more financial detail you need depends on what you plan to do with your business plan. If you intend to use it to seek financing from a bank, you want as much financial detail as possible. If you aren't number savvy, it pays to have an accountant put these spreadsheets together for you; banks are very impressed by realistic, detailed financials.

If your business plan is mainly to guide you in the growth of your business, then you can decide how much financial detail you want to estimate up front.

This is all a lot of work to put together, no question. But it is definitely worth it, if for no other reason than to clarify your business framework in your mind and guide you as you proceed from a great idea to opening your doors.

Startup Costs

You want to have a pretty good handle on your projected startup costs before you get to Day 1: Thinking Through the Details. This is something you want to have in your business plan. Costs depend a great deal on the kind of gift business you are starting. You need to know

- → *inventory costs.* How much you plan to order for opening inventory, what kind of discounts you can get from suppliers as a new customer, and what kind of product you are selling are the key factors in figuring out your startup costs. What kind of item—for instance, jewelry compared to Beanie Babies—and what level of quality within that category—custom-made jewelry with precious stones compared to Timex watches with Velcro wristbands, for example—are factors.
- → *your advertising and marketing needs.* How much do you have to do to get the attention of your customers?
- → *website creation and branding considerations such as a company logo.*

Don't skimp on the marketing and advertising. If no one knows about your online gift business, you won't have any sales! Generating traffic to your site is your key to success. You can do this yourself and in Chapter 6 you will learn how.

SWOT Analysis

In considering your overall online gift business idea, a common business tool to use is SWOT Analysis. SWOT stands for Strengths, Weaknesses, Opportunities, and Threats. These categories cover the following:

➡ *Strengths*. Things that make your business different from your competitors' businesses. This includes you and your personal experience.

➡ *Weaknesses*. Things that you need to work on to get up to snuff for your business and that your competitors could take advantage of until you overcome them.

➡ *Opportunities*. What might benefit your company right now.

➡ *Threats*. What do your competitors' have that you don't? What other things can harm the success of your business?

Brainstorm at least a couple items in each category that apply to your idea. And put this analysis in your business plan.

Where the Money Comes From

Most online startups use personal savings to begin. Traditional financing for an online gift business can be difficult to obtain, but there are other ways to raise money to get started.

➡ *Your own resources*. Do a thorough inventory of your assets. People generally have more assets than they immediately realize. These assets could include savings accounts, equity in real estate, retirement accounts, vehicles, recreation equipment, collections, and other investments. You may opt to sell assets for cash or use them as collateral for a loan. Also take a look at your personal line of credit. Many successful businesses have been started with credit cards. But be careful with all of these. You don't want to drain yourself so you have no cushion at all.

➡ *Friends and family*. The next logical step after gathering your own resources is to approach friends and relatives who believe in you and want to help you succeed. Be cautious with these arrangements; no matter how close you are, be professional. Put everything in writing, and be sure the individuals you approach can afford to take the risk of investing in your business.

➡ *Partners*. Is there someone who may want to team up with you in your venture? Maybe someone who has financial resources and wants to work side by side with you in the business? Or perhaps someone who has money to invest but no interest in doing the actual work? If you go this route, be sure to create a written partnership agreement that clearly defines your respective responsibilities and obligations.

➡ *Government programs.* Take advantage of the abundance of local, state, and federal programs designed to support small businesses. Make your first stop the U.S. Small Business Administration, then investigate various other programs. Women, minorities, and veterans should check out niche financing possibilities designed to help these groups get into business. An online search should lead you to plenty of options.

Your Gift Business: The Specifics

Once you have a grasp of starting a business in general, it's time to think about your business specifically. You've probably been thinking about this online gift business idea for a while. So it shouldn't be too hard to make a decision about exactly what you want to sell before you settle in to the nitty gritty of pulling it all together in a week. This is one of the most important decisions you will make prelaunch. You can always add to your offerings, but what you decide to sell will have an impact on the design of your website, how you order your inventory, where you store your inventory, and right on down to the type of packaging you purchase to ship orders to your customers. As you can imagine, choosing jewelry vs. smoked salmon vs. decorative spun glassware will result in very different general requirements when it comes to the details of running your business. So, before Day 1, what do you want to sell?

CLICK TIP

Once you are down to the nitty gritty of actually getting online and up and running, doing it in a week is definitely feasible. But plan to spend as much as six months of research time leading up to that one intense week.

Decisions, Decisions

Maybe you already know what gift line you are interested in. Perhaps your favorite hobby has been a potential business for years—good for you for finally taking the plunge! There's no better time than now to make use of this computerized world and the commercial potential it offers.

To help you in your decisions, take a moment to answer the questions in the sidebar in this chapter. You want to go into this venture with your eyes wide open. Things sometimes don't work out as you want, but the chances of being successful and happy with your choice are much better if you think everything through before making important decisions.

KEY QUESTIONS TO ASK YOURSELF

Ask yourself the following questions before you lock in to a specific gift category:

1. What about this category interests you enough that you think it will sustain you for the long haul?

2. What in your background makes you familiar enough with the category—a serious hobby, previous work experience, etc.—to be able to create a viable source of gift items?

3. What expansion potential does the category have to keep your business growing over the years?

4. If you choose this category for online gift sales, what does your day-to-day life look like? Is it a life you could envision enjoying?

5. What parts of the business do not appeal to you? Can you think of ways to delegate these or set up the business to make them have less of an impact or take less of your time?

6. Where do you envision yourself five years from now?

Online Gift Business Ideas

Almost anything is fair game for an online gift business. The most common for startups are hobby-related, knowledge-related, and artisan. Each general type of online gift business has some unique aspects to consider when designing an online store. They are covered in a later chapter.

Hobby-Related

Do you have a hobby that you enjoy that would be a perfect segue into a business venture? The possibilities are endless, from horseback riding to scrapbooking to photography to rock climbing to stamp collecting, sewing, knitting, woodworking, gardening, aquariums, you name it. You can sell supplies needed to do the hobby, books covering how-to information, kits, equipment, and so on. In the case of something like horseback riding, there is equipment for the rider, equipment for the horse, and everyday and health care needs for the horse. The additional advantage of creating a business surrounding your hobby is that you get to buy your own supplies and related items at a discount!

Knowledge-Related

Are you a professional in a particular field? For instance, are you an accountant, a plumber, an architect, a chef, an interior designer, or a wedding photographer? Start selling your knowledge online. People are always looking for unique gifts. As a plumber, you could create gift certificates for housewarming or newlywed gifts. An interior designer could have an online gift business of unique lamps and other home accessories. A chef's online gift business could entail cookbooks, specialty food items, and other yummy edible gifts.

Artisan

If you are skilled at creating products, an online gift business may be just the thing you need to boost your skill to the next level. Many artists such as jewelers and painters spend more time than they want to setting up accounts and supplying retail stores. Instead, with an online shop, you don't have to spend your creative time doing business, you can do the business end of things on your own schedule.

The Name Game

Naming your business is another task you want to accomplish before day one of your seven-day business creation adventure. What you choose for a business name is always extremely important, even more so when it comes to an online business. You will need to use your business name with everything you do.

First, your business name has a lot to do with whether and where in line your business comes up when someone searches your category. If a potential customer goes online and searches for "equine gifts" and your business's name is Equine Gifts—voila! Your business will most likely appear pretty high up on the returned list of websites, if not first. But if that potential customer searches "equine gifts" and your business name is Trigger's Finds—well, let's just say "equine gifts" is probably going to have to be every other phrase in your website for search engines to pull up your business early in the list this potential customer gets.

The other unique characteristic of an online business is that you are never standing there in front of your potential customer with a ready explanation. If customers go in a retail shop not quite knowing what the shop sells, it takes just a minute for them to get a good idea—added to the fact that a clerk will be in the vicinity armed with the info needed to explain the shop if need be.

You can do that online once you get your customer to your website, but one key difference is that when a person is walking down Main Street looking for a gift, there are only so many shops to go into. On the internet, the shop selection is quite literally endless—e-Main Street consists of the entire world!

WARNING

Don't get too cute with your online name. Shoppers online are shopping the world over—you have enough competition without losing potential customers because they can't figure out what you are!

So you need to give yourself as much of an edge as possible, and your name is where you start.

Once you narrow your possibilities, do a search online to see if another business is already using that name. If one is, you can still use the name, but you will probably not be able to use it as your domain name. Chances are the other online store is already doing that.

Take some time with this naming thing. Bring a few friends in on your choices and get their feedback as potential customers. Quiz them about the names of the gift sites they visit. Once you begin to market your business name, it is pretty tough to change it.

Unlike a retail storefront operation, you don't have to be as concerned with how the name rolls off your tongue when you answer the phone. However, it should be easy to spell. Strange spellings of common words can work or not—they may make your name memorable or they may mean no one finds you. If your name is E-Kwhine, people aren't going to come up with it when they plug "Equine" into their browser.

Inventory Research

The ordering process comes in Day 2: Focus on Inventory, but by the time you get to that point, you should be armed with sources for acquiring your inventory. Have some manufacturer research already done in your gift category. Chances are if this is an area you already know from either previous work experience or your own personal interests, you already know some of the players. But if you are to stand out in the crowd—and every category online has a crowd—you need to be searching for unique items that no one else is carrying. Remembering you for having things they haven't seen elsewhere is what will drive people back to your site.

You can add unique items later after you have your site up and running. But in order to intrigue potential customers, you need to have some unique items right from the start. Don't create a mundane online store, tell customers that your site will become more fascinating as time goes by, and expect them to believe it. They need to see that you have a sharp eye for unique products; the only way to have them believe that is to prove it.

Sources

Where you get your inventory will have a lot to do with what kind of profit margin you can expect to have. Here are some typical sources:

➡ *Local craftspeople.* Local craftspeople can be a source of unique items since buyers in Milwaukee, Wisconsin, probably do not have knowledge of local crafters in Portsmouth, New Hampshire. This can provide you with some great items to make your offerings different from the rest.

➡ *Wholesalers.* Wholesalers are where you will probably get your best discounts. They are designed specifically to buy inventory in large quantity from suppliers at high discounts in order to extend discounts to resellers like you. You often need to buy in sufficient quantities, and get increasing discounts for increasing numbers.

➡ *Online sites.* eBay, Craigslist, or Overstock.com can have some interesting items at good prices, but remember that all of your potential customers have access to these sites and it is time consuming to use them to purchase your inventory.

➡ *Garage sales, yard sales, flea markets, and other "used stores."* This means of inventory acquisition also is time consuming. But while a yard sale is open to everyone, you can make these yard sale items accessible to the world. This can be a great way to enhance your offerings and entice customers to keep coming back to see what unique items you have. For instance, if you are selling horse-related items and have different one-of-a-kind horse-related items on your site each week, horse enthusiasts will come back looking for what's new.

➡ *Trade shows.* You should plan to attend general gift-related trade shows and trade shows related to your specific gift category. These are places where if you look carefully and look beyond the companies shouting the loudest, you can find unique and interesting products to add to your line. Of course, don't avoid those big companies doing all the major promotions at the show; your customers expect you to have the run-of-the-mill stuff along with unique stuff. Both will keep them coming back.

➡ *Importers.* You should be enticing customers back with different inventory all the time, even if it's new and produced en masse. Importers are a great way to find unique items that are not being offered by every gift website on the internet.

➡ *Local manufacturers.* Local manufacturers may not provide you with unique items because they are manufacturing for the whole country or world, and just happen to be located near you. But you could be able to get their products at better prices. At the least, you avoid shipping charges if you can pick them up yourself.

Ordering

Your actual ordering will be explained in Chapter 3. You can do most of this over the internet. But even if you are computer savvy and starting an online store, having print catalogs to order from can be more convenient. They allow you to flag the products you are interested in ordering, compare products among various catalogs, and see where you stand in how purchase totals relate to the amount you have budgeted for startup inventory. On the internet, you can go through the process and end up losing your shopping cart before you are ready to place your final order. Many online catalogs require you to set up an account before you can begin loading your shopping cart, which is time consuming, especially if in the end you find you don't plan to order from them anyway. You can still order online once you have all your ducks in a row via print catalogs.

Storage

Before you begin to have inventory shipped to you, you need to sort out where you are going to store your inventory. You should have storage in place before Day 1. This should be the same place where you are going to pack goods to ship out. It would be best to have a place where couriers can pick up your shipments, so consider whether you need space with a loading dock or at least one with access for the size truck you need given the size of shipments you plan to have going out the door.

It is possible to lease space within a larger warehouse. That gives you the ability to have deliveries accepted while you are not at the warehouse location.

Be sure to put in your lease contract that you don't want to pay extra for wages to employees to receive your goods. They don't have to stock the shelves, you can do that at your own convenience. Just be sure you are able to get into the space at odd hours so it truly can be at your convenience.

You can have your deliveries made to your home if you want. You can even have your warehouse at your home, but you do need a convenient, effective, and efficient storage space.

If you decide to have storage at your home, you need to check local zoning laws to be sure you can have a homebased business—and one that can have big delivery trucks coming and going several times a day. One of the reasons zoning is put in place is to avoid commercial traffic in residential areas where children are playing and balls are rolling into the streets.

Shipping Details

You will want to have your shipping details figured out before you have to send out your first order (which you hope is on the first day you are in business!). Make sure you know your shipper(s), have the right containers, and have sufficient paper supplies.

As far as shippers go, UPS, FedEx, and the United States Postal Service (USPS) are the most common carriers. Your choices will depend on what you are shipping. Most of these carriers have online tracking systems allowing you or your customer to know where an order is at any given moment. This service costs money, so you don't want to charge a disproportionate tracking fee to send out a few sticks of gum. But if you are shipping diamond jewelry, you want tracking and insurance, and the customer will be happy to pay for it. And don't forget, except for USPS, most carriers do not ship to a post office box.

Have the right kind of containers on hand to ship your items so orders arrive at their destination in the same condition that they left your warehouse. This means appropriate-size

GIFTS.COM

Self-dubbed as "the easy way to find great gifts," gifts.com is an online gift-searching site that helps people find what they are looking for. The site is organized by category, occasion, and even personality ("achievers," "divas"). You can register as a merchant and pay a fee for leads it sends to your site.

cartons, padding, and adequate sealing for the package. If you sell items of many different weights and sizes, you may have several different options for shipping containers.

Buy a supply of paper for printing invoices and packing slips, and purchase mailing labels either preprinted with your return address or computer-ready for you to print yourself. You want to look professional. But don't get into having cartons preprinted with your name on it or that kind of thing. It is unnecessary and expensive.

Infrastructure

Just like any business, you need to have professionals lined up to help you with the "back office" side of things. Perhaps you want to do your own day-to-day bookkeeping, but unless you have solid accounting experience, be sure to hire an accountant to do your books quarterly and help you keep up with taxes. This person will be invaluable when you get to the point of whether or not to expand your business.

You will also need a legal team, even if it means just having a lawyer you can call to help when something comes up. Don't think you will never need a lawyer—having someone who is familiar with you and your business already lined up when something arises makes things go a whole lot better. You will already know that this is someone you can work with and won't have to find out you are incompatible with the lawyer you picked at the last minute to deal with a legal issue at hand.

CLICK TIP

The Small Business Administration's website (sba.gov) contains lots of information to help with business infrastructure decisions. Also look at the SCORE site. At SCORE retired business professionals offer advice and guidance to small business startups (score.org). And check out Entrepreneur's site (entrepreneur.com). These sites will help you make sure you have covered the details.

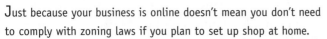

WARNING

Just because your business is online doesn't mean you don't need to comply with zoning laws if you plan to set up shop at home. Zoning laws are designed so that areas of a city or town stick to their intended atmosphere of either residential, commercial, or a specific mix.

Website Designers

Before you leave this planning phase, you should be sure to have a website designer lined up. On Day 1 we are going to review everything you need to plan the design of your site and you are going to begin working with the designer to create just what you need.

Designing online stores is not rocket science nor is it uncharted territory. You should pick a designer that is within your price range and can deliver a smart, competent, attractive website design within a few days. This should not be impossible. Or you may decide the best way to go is with a turnkey template that allows some customization.

To do either you need to have done your research and found a designer who can work within your time and money parameters, with whom you think you can have a good working rapport, and who you think understands what you are looking for in a website. Or find a turnkey operation that works for your business.

Business Startup Checklist

Here's an overview of the actions you need to take for effective startup. Not all of these steps are necessary. They depend on the type of business you plan to launch and what you will ultimately be selling. In addition, the order in which you complete these tasks may vary. By the end of the seven-day program presented here, you should have all the key steps completed.

☐ Develop a list of potential products to sell, and research them.
☐ Determine your target customer base.

- ❏ Create a detailed business plan (in writing).
- ❏ Brainstorm a name for your business.
- ❏ Obtain the computer equipment, internet access, software, and business equipment and supplies you need to get started.
- ❏ Register your business with your local and state government and the IRS. (This step might include incorporating your business or setting up a DBA.)
- ❏ Establish the infrastructure of your business, including your bookkeeping practices.
- ❏ Develop a realistic budget and raise the startup money needed to launch your business.
- ❏ Register one or more domain names (.com).
- ❏ Research e-commerce turnkey solutions and find one that meets your needs and start using it.
- ❏ Research sources for acquiring the product you wish to sell, including distributors, manufacturers, wholesalers, importers, and so on.
- ❏ Create detailed product descriptions and acquire professional-quality photos of the products you plan to sell.
- ❏ Gather all of the content and additional assets you'll incorporate into your website.
- ❏ Create a company logo and the other graphic assets you plan to incorporate into your website.
- ❏ Develop a strategy to process online payments, such as obtaining a merchant account and/or registering as a merchant with PayPal and/or Google Checkout.
- ❏ Develop and launch a detailed, multifaceted marketing, advertising, promotional, and public relations campaign.
- ❏ Acquire an ample supply of product inventory to get started, and develop business relationships with your key suppliers.
- ❏ Hire freelancers to help you plan, develop, launch, and maintain your website, and operate your business.
- ❏ Research and analyze your potential competition.
- ❏ Create your website and add all of the functionality you'll need to effectively sell your product.

❑ Before launching your website, test it carefully and ensure it contains no dead links, typographical errors, or other problems.

❑ Hire website testers and have them thoroughly test your entire website looking for typos, dead links, and other problems.

❑ Establish your business's policies and operational procedures, including how you'll approach customer service.

❑ Create your company's shipping department and develop detailed procedures for promptly and accurately fulfilling orders.

❑ Focus on getting your site listed with search engines and then focus on search engine optimization.

❑ Carefully monitor all aspects of your business and fine-tune your operational procedures and practices as necessary.

❑ Track the success of all marketing, advertising, and promotional efforts, and fine-tune your strategies to generate the most traffic to your site possible while incurring the lowest possible expense.

❑ Start planning how you'll expand your online business in the future.

Chapter 2

Day 1:
Thinking Through
the Details

*N*ow you are ready to begin the nitty gritty details of getting your online gift business up and running. By the end of Day 7, you will be ready for your first order! But make yourself a pot of strong coffee, there's a lot to do before then.

Here's what you will do on Day 1:

➡ Learn how to target your audience with the right marketing message.

➡ Put your competitive research to use.

➡ Figure out your website design.

➡ Hand your website design ideas to the designer.

➡ Learn what you are going to have to do to attract visitors to your website.

Targeting Your Audience

Now that you know what you are going to sell, you need to figure out how to target your audience. You know who that audience is—between deciding on your gift category and writing your business plan, you've figured that out. Now you need to get your website to their attention and get it on their "favorites" list.

Right now, though, you will just be planning your marketing attack. You don't want to pull the trigger until you have your site up and running. When your target market sees your enticing message they need to be able to go to it the minute they get your message and they also need to be able to place their "can't-wait" order right then while on your site. They can't run into "under construction" messages that deter them from ever coming back. Think about how many times you've considered buying tickets to something but the tickets don't go on sale for another two weeks. By then you will have forgotten, lost your enthusiasm for it, committed your money to something else, or scheduled something else for that date. It's the same with your customers. Their interest is now.

Gift purchases are often impulse purchases. They are also often "gift for self" purchases. So be ready when your potential customer is, and turn a potential sale into an actual sale.

How do you entice gift purchases? Your message needs to convey some key benefits:

➡ The benefit to the gift buyer is that she or he will look good in the eyes of the receiver—the receiver will think of the giver as generous, astute, or having good taste. Seldom is a gift giver making the purchase simply to make someone else happy. It also represents something about the giver.

➡ Sometimes the benefit to the buyer is simply to fulfill an obligation, such as a wedding gift, a baby shower gift, or a birthday gift. Convey

CLICK TIP

Consider using eBay stores or Yahoo! stores to start your online gift business and try out your concept. You will get a complete walk-through on how to do this through the websites. When you are ready and feel the concept can be a thriving business, you can launch your independent site. Or alternatively, you can decide the concept doesn't work and either tweak it or shut it down without having spent oodles of money.

the message that this is OK, that fulfilling an obligation can still make the giver feel good.

➡ Sometimes the purchaser is buying a gift for himself or herself. Convey the message that not only is that OK, it is encouraged!

➡ The buyer is looking for easy purchasing. Your marketing message needs to get the point across that nothing could be easier than purchasing from your website.

Online Research of Competitors

You have done research on web competitors to create your business plan, and now is the time to put that research to use. One thing this competition research should have done at the business planning stage is to help you weed out gift business ideas that you discovered probably could not be successful. While pet rocks might have been a craze in the '70s, setting up a whole business selling designer clothing for pet rocks is probably not going to be a moneymaking venture. Sure, you might be able to spark a mini-revival, but it will be shortlived and the money you make probably won't cover your website creation costs let alone provide you with any meaningful income.

So what did you see that was successful? Don't look just at gift sites. Look at websites in the category you have chosen to sell in. For instance, if you are starting an online equine gift shop, look at other equine-related sites. This will help you see how people interested in horses expect things to look. There are western riding styles and English riding styles—an equine gift business would probably want to cater to both. How do you do that? And what about kids—are those horse-loving preteen girls going to be part of your market? That requires a completely different approach. The good news is that you can create an overall "equine" theme to your website and visitors can click on different pages that are of interest to them specifically. And those pages can carry your basic look while also being specifically geared to the western rider or the young horse enthusiast.

You should have come to this stage with your gift category in place—riders, golfers, motorcyclists, doll lovers, cat lovers, or general gift items—so now you will be looking for implementation. Here are some questions to ask while you look over gift websites and sites in the category you have chosen:

- How do the successful websites look?
- What are they offering for discounts, incentives, and specials?
- How does the site's design match the type of item that is being sold?
- Are there bells and whistles that seem necessary to selling in that category?
- Are there bells and whistles that seem unnecessary?

Your competitive research should have told you a lot about how to design your website. Now you need to get ready to give good advice to your designer, who you have lined up already in the preplanning stage. The designer should know you are ready to begin the website design phase with the intention of getting to the launch phase in a week.

CLICK TIP

Once you have determined your target audience, you need to do everything you can to familiarize yourself with that audience.

Interview anyone you know personally who fits the profile—women age 28–39 with children, divorced men age 47 and up with grown children, women age 30–40 with no children. Read the magazines that they read, look at the websites they look at, go to the bookstores and browse the kind of books they would browse. Even if you are a member of your target audience, learn about the audience beyond you.

Website Design

What do you need to hand to your website designer to get him or her started? There are several things you will want to provide for your designer to do the best job at creating the website you want.

➡ One thing your designer needs is a good sense of the style you want in your website. Should it be understated and elegant? Loud, bright, and busy? Somewhere in between? This is where your research of your target market comes into play. What do the people you intend to be your customers want to see when they get to your site?

➡ Let the designer know what kind of movement you want customers to be able to do. Should they see multiple products when they arrive at your homepage? Or will they need to read exciting marketing copy to entice them to drill down into your site and see all you have to offer?

➡ Figure out what buttons you want along the edge of the site. A "home" button often brings visitors to the page they would come to if they search your domain name. You should also plan to have a FAQs (frequently asked questions) section. Always include a "contact" button so customers can easily find the information they need to contact you by e-mail, phone, and snail mail. In the retail business, you definitely need a "returns" button. This outlines your returns policy. Many customers want to know your policy upfront before deciding whether to make a purchase or not.

> **GLOSSARY**
>
> *Assets*: Design elements used in website creation.

Turnkey Solutions

You may decide to do your own website. You can do it from scratch, although to do a decent one you need to know some web coding. If you do or if you are willing and eager to learn, go for it! If you don't, consider using one of the many template options that are available for relatively little money.

These templates are turnkey operations. You pick and choose from a menu of designs, fonts, layouts, etc. You can customize colors. And then you plug your product photos into the template.

Template services usually offer hosting services along with their design services. Some of the templates are even free of charge if you use hosting service for a monthly charge. They also develop forms of online payment for your site. They have numerous advantages including:

- ➡ Startup costs are modest, especially compared to having a commerce website designed from scratch.
- ➡ They provide all of the development tools, soup to nuts.
- ➡ You do not need to know any programming.
- ➡ They typically offers dozens, perhaps hundreds, of designs with mix-and-match options and customizing features that mean your site won't look like anyone else's even though it is from a template.
- ➡ They are compatible with all the common tools you'll want to use such as accounting software, inventory management, and database software, and shipping records.

Several companies offer turnkey website solutions. Each one offers numerous options. Their slightly different packages mean that you want to research them carefully and choose the group of features that best suits the online gift business you are starting. For example, for a site that will sell fewer than 20 items, GoDaddy has a Quick Shopping Cart Economy edition for under $10 a month that will serve your purpose well. You can step up to a Deluxe Edition, which of course costs more but allows you to show and sell up to 100 products.

You should plan to thoroughly investigate eBay, which has numerous possibilities for online selling, including eBay stores.

FREELANCERS

You can probably find freelancers right in your area who are capable of producing good copy for your website. There are also other places you can look, such as elance.com, for skilled website copywriters.

Customizing Your Website

There are some elements of your website that are original material that you either create or pay to have created for your business. These include

➡ *a logo*. You can create this yourself but it is often better to spend a little money and have this professionally designed.

➡ *product descriptions*. Each of the items on your site needs to be described. Read lots and lots of online gift sites and pick a style that projects the image you want to project. Write the product descriptions yourself or, if you are not comfortable with writing, hire someone to write them for you. Be sure to have a written contract with that person so that the material is clearly owned by your business. You also want to be sure to have a third party read over the product descriptions to see if they make sense, match the actual product features, and include the details that will be important to potential customers.

➡ *other written material*. You probably also want to have a description of your business, perhaps something about yourself, and some information on returns and other procedural details that need to be written by you or by someone else.

➡ *photos*. If you have a good digital camera, by all means learn how to take quality photos of your gift items to put on your website. You probably have access to product photos from many of your suppliers.

WARNING

Do not infringe on copyrights and trademarks! Any material—text, graphics, photos, video, audio, animation, logos—that you did not personally create needs *written permission* for you to use it. If you'll be using product artwork/photos or product descriptions created by the manufacturer of the product you're selling, for example, make sure you have permission to use these materials before incorporating them into your website (and, further, make sure the manufacturer has the right to give you permission for material created by someone else).

Selling from a Website

There was a time when small businesses used websites mainly as marketing pieces—people came to the site to view your products, then either called an order in or printed out a order form from the site and faxed their order to you. Those days are pretty much gone. Customers expect to be able to sit at their computer and not only see what you have to offer but be able to order it right then and there. If they can't, there is a good chance you are going to lose them to another gift site where they can.

The two key things that your site will need—and that your designer will set you up with—is a shopping cart for customers to collect their items in and a secure way to pay for them.

Shopping Cart

The shopping cart is a simple function that your web designer can build into your site if you say you want it (which you do). As your online customers shop, they can click the little button that says "add this item to my shopping cart" and the product will join the list of other items they have already put in the cart. Some carts accumulate items that stay there even after the customer leaves the site. This feature can translate into more sales—if customers get interrupted before completing the transaction, they don't have to go through the entire shopping process when they return to your site. "Abandoned" shopping carts is a big issue with online shopping—customers leave before the sale is done—and this feature can retrieve some of those abandoned carts.

CLICK TIP

If at all possible, create a shopping cart that can be saved. One of the biggest online shopping problems is abandoned shopping carts—the customer goes to all the trouble of shopping and putting things in her cart and then, for whatever reason, leaves your site and the contents of her cart end up in the cyberspace dump. Being able to get back to a partially full shopping cart is one way to entice customers back to your site to keep shopping and complete their purchase.

The shopping cart page is where customers can make changes. Here they can change the quantity of each item (sometimes bad for you, when they decide to change it to 0, other times good when they decide not only will they order one of these bracelets for their sister but make it three and they'll send one to Mom and Aunt Jean as well).

The shopping cart page is also where customers decide what kind of shipping they want. Always offer inexpensive shipping options along with overnight options. The shipping charge is one of those things that still bogs down catalog and online sales, so give customers the option of making it very cheap. But you also want them to feel they can shop online at the last minute as well, so the ability to have something shipped overnight is a must.

CLICK TIP

If you choose to go with one of the turnkey solutions for your startup online business, plan to research other options for the future. If your business is successful, you will probably outgrow the template solutions and their menu of offerings.

Payment Options

Anyone reading this has shopped online and knows that credit cards are always an option for paying for your cyberpurchase. While using credit cards online has become very secure, there are still people who have no interest in giving out their credit card number over the internet. Some companies still give those people the option of faxing or calling in their order—both good reasons to make sure your contact information is available on all web pages.

PayPal is another option for paying online. People with a PayPal account load it up with funds and then funds are withdrawn when you use it to pay for a purchase online. PayPal payments are essentially electronic withdrawals from a checking account, allowing you to send money to anyone

---

CLICK TIP

You may think you don't need a FAQs (frequently asked questions) page on your website, but you would be surprised the number of e-mails and phone calls you can prevent just by having a place for people to get simple questions answered. Keep track of your calls and e-mails you get and consider adding answers to these queries to your FAQs section. If one or two people have the query, so do others.

---

with an e-mail address. PayPal became the payment method of choice for eBay traders, so much so that in 2002 eBay bought PayPal. If you allow PayPal for purchases, your site will include a PayPal button.

More on these payment options will be covered in a later chapter.

Marketing Your Website

Once you have created your website, you can't keep it a secret! You need to spend as much time marketing your website as you do creating, maintaining, and updating it. Your competition is the whole world of the internet, so you have a lot of marketing to do. Your website is your link to the entire world of customers, so shout it from the rooftops.

Be sure your web address is on every printed piece you create for your business—letterhead, business cards, gift enclosures, print advertisements, newsletters, radio ads; everything that has to do with your business should announce your web address. Put the address in your answering machine message. If you have a retail store, make sure your website address is somewhere

---

CLICK TIP

Always include your business's name, address, phone number, and e-mail address on every page of your website. Once customers have drilled a few pages down into your site, they don't want to have to backtrack all the way back to your homepage just to get your contact information.

GET PEOPLE CLICKING

There's no point to having a website if you don't do what you can to get people to click on it. Here are some tips for attracting visitors, and possibly buyers, to your website:

- Tell all your friends and family and ask them to tell all their friends and family.

- Do the appropriate search engine registration.

- Make sure every printed and online piece you send to anyone has your website URL listed prominently.

- Suggest visitors bookmark your site.

- Trade web advertising with other websites.

- Create contests with giveaways.

- Change your content/product regularly to keep people coming back to see what's new.

- Join online discussion groups.

- If you do public speaking, always mention your site.

- Provide an "expert" column to newspapers and make sure to mention your website in your bio.

These are just a few of a long list of ideas for getting people to come to your website in the first place, keep coming back, and encourage them to tell everyone they know.

WARNING

Be sure to set up your website so old products can be removed and new ones can be dropped in with ease. You will want to change your product offering regularly, at least weekly. You don't want it to be such a chore that you are tempted not to bother.

on the door so anyone walking by who either doesn't have time to come in or wanders by during your off hours knows they can find you on the internet.

Putting the "Gift" in a Gift Business

Creating an online gift business has many similarities to and many differences from a brick-and-mortar gift store. Let's start with the similarities.

You are selling things that people use their disposable income to purchase. Therefore, whether you have a retail store or an online site, you need to appeal to potential customer's emotions. However, keep in mind that they need what you have a little more than if they were just purchasing it for themselves—many times they are trying to fulfill an obligation of a shower gift, holiday gift, hostess gift, or whatever.

You need to direct people in how your items can fulfill their gift-giving need. This is a little harder to do online than in person, but it needs to be done. Online gift retailers need to become expert with creating marketing copy that directs people to their need being fulfilled.

Brick-and-mortar retail and online shopping can have differences as well. Although both types of selling need to offer customers choices, retailers can fill their shop with seemingly unrelated items and allow customers to walk around and discover things. While the online gift shop can hold an infinite number of products, compared to the brick-and-mortar store, it can't be cluttered. You'll want to group things and give them categories to help lead

---

CLICK TIP

If you are selling gifts that require the owner to know how to use them, be sure to include all the technical details in your product descriptions. If you don't know how to use the item—say you have a category of power tools on your site and you don't even know how to plug one in—enlist someone who does know to try out these tools for you and help you decide what needs to go in the write-up. You don't have to hire these people; they could be friends and family who would be happy to do it for a nice discount on your site.

---

shoppers to products. The groupings may be general—"baby items" or "pet items"—but they can't just be part of an overall general mix or no one is going to find them online.

Gift Category Ideas

Limitless categories exist to specialize in for your online gift business. While not 100 percent necessary, it is best if you choose a category that you are actually interested in, not just one that you think would be successful. You may find that your interest in running the business fades quickly if you are not interested in the topic or products in your chosen specialization. And you will be better able to talk with customers about products if you know the category—you will be able to speak with more enthusiasm and credibility if you are, say, a motorcycle rider yourself and are helping people pick out gifts for their motorcycling enthusiast family member from your online motorcycle gift line. The following 20 ideas are just a few that might trigger your own creativity in coming up with a gift category that will work for you.

1. Wedding

The wedding industry is so big that wedding presents are a huge subniche of this already huge category. There are approximately 2.5 million weddings per year in the United States and an average of 175 invited guests to those weddings (Chris Jaeger, "Book More Weddings," weddingindustrystatistics.com). Even if only half of those guests buy the bride and groom a gift, that is one boatload of wedding gift purchases that need fulfilling! Why not make sure they come to your online gift site to do that?

The wedding gift category can be tricky because you need to consider that not all weddings are first-time weddings and not all participants are young couples in their twenties—you may consider a different kind of gift for these different kinds of brides and grooms. However, there are many old standbys that can be tweaked a bit to fulfill almost any need. Being creative is going to work in your favor.

Take cookbooks, for example. A traditional cookbook gift would be a classic like *Joy of Cooking* or *The Fannie Farmer Cookbook*. But these days, there are other types of cookbooks that are going to be popular with a new lifestyle—grilling cookbooks for those that have learned that you can keep your grill going even through a northeast winter! Or cookbooks that cater to a healthier meal. Or that cater to the busy couple with one-dish meals or soup/salad cookbooks or even cookbooks for that comeback appliance, the slow cooker.

Wedding gift registries have become very popular—be sure to offer one so that gift buyers can come to your site and easily pick out something the wedding couple actually wants. And even if your site is not specifically directed toward wedding gifts, any gift site can benefit from a wedding registry.

2. Baby

Like wedding gifts, baby showers are still in full swing. According to the National Center for Health Statistics, well over four million babies were born in the United States in 2006. Like weddings, that represents a lot of potential gifts!

With the baby gift category, you can choose to specialize. Clothing is always a sure bet when it comes to kids—parents love to get children's clothing as gifts because babies grow out of them so fast that they are a constant need. Another popular category these days is safety items—special cribs, safety equipment for the home such as kitchen cupboard locks and electrical outlet covers, safe strollers. Whether you focus on safety items or not, be sure everything you offer for baby falls under all of the government safety regulations for the different age groups.

Also, handmade baby items from blankets to hats never go out of style. You can start by specializing in one category and adding categories as you expand. Or your offerings can run the gamut, with your specialty being high quality.

3. Jewelry

Jewelry is a perfect item for the online gift website. The items are typically small and can be shipped relatively inexpensively. The one thing that you do need to take into consideration, however, is insurance. Depending on the type of jewelry you plan to sell, it is important not to send it out the door without the proper level of insurance.

The jewelry category overall certainly has its own specialties—handcrafted, silver, gold, precious gems, antique or estate jewelry. And from there you can specialize in rings, necklaces, pins, bracelets, body jewelry. Or you can offer gold jewelry in all those categories. Jewelry tends to show well in photos on websites. Although you need to be careful of glare and shadows, most jewelry photos easily on handsome backdrops such as purple, red, or black satin or velvet fabric.

4. Pets

Here is a category it is hard to go wrong with these days! With approximately 75 millions dogs and 89 million cats in U.S. households (according to 2007-2008 statistics compiled by the American Pet Products Manufacturers Association), it shouldn't be too hard to attract a few pet owners to your online gift store. People are always giving gifts to their pets, and anyone who owns a pet knows that many of the gifts they receive from others revolve around their interest in pets. People are making a living on online sites devoted to single types of pets, such as Scottie dogs—Campbell's Scottish Terriers (campbellscotties.com) sells everything from salt and pepper shakers to Christmas cards to soaps with Scottie dogs pictured on them. Anyone who owns a Scottie would be thrilled with any gift from Campbell's Scottish Terriers. Coon cats, quarter horses, hedgehogs—you name it, people and their pets are nuts about pet-related gifts. You can also be more practical by selling handmade leashes or homecooked pet treats. Or be more creative by selling pet-focused art and even pet portraits.

5. Baskets

Gift baskets are the perfect gift item to sell online. It is so easy to set up your site to allow customers to mix and match items or to offer specialty categories—or both! Baskets can be offered in several sizes and are so much fun to create. For those who want to make it simple and be able to just click on a ready-made basket and tell you where to send it, be sure to promote the ease with which someone can send a very special gift from your website. Or you can pick up on any of the categories mentioned here—pets, baby, nautical, food—and offer a selection of items to create any size basket the buyer wishes. Several things to keep in mind with gift baskets include making sure you have the right size shipping cartons on hand for the types of baskets you offer; being careful to anchor your items in the basket so it arrives looking like you intended it to; and paying attention to any foodstuffs you include such as not packaging food items with scented soaps or candles and not using perishable food.

6. Green

The environmental movement has come full circle—no longer a cult movement, "going green" is happening around every corner. You could go green with a gift website! Who's to say giving someone a carton of energy-saving compact fluorescent light bulbs isn't a great gift item! Offer a newlyweds gift of a carton full of green housecleaning products. Sell clothing made from organic fibers or books about how to save the planet. Not only can you sell green gifts, but you could work on making your company green, too. Green businesses are becoming so prevalent, there are even consultants popping up who can assess your company for its green quotient and offer environmentally friendly tips.

7. Books

Books are a perennial great gift item. The key to having a great website for giving books as gifts is to categorize your selection, making it easy for buyers to consider a book for the gardener, sailor, knitter, new parent, or mystery lover on their gift list. Consider offering free gift wrapping—books are about the easiest item to gift wrap that there is. It is a great added value service. Offer a few different wrapping paper selections and show them on your site. As with any of these categories, it is easy to set up a wish list service and purchasers can pick off a registry to get just the right book.

8. Country

Country style will never go out of style. And there is enough country to go around that anyone could make a go of an online business offering country-style items. For a gift business, you won't want to offer furniture or other big-ticket personal taste items. But that leaves plenty to choose from. From lamps to lampshades, trinkets and knickknacks, throw rugs, artwork, you name it—country style can be had in almost everything. Those looking to give a gift to someone with a country-decorated home will look to your site to help them find just the right item. And what fun it will be shopping around the manufacturer and wholesaler sites to find new product to offer.

9. Nautical

Sailors love their boats. And sailors are often given gifts of all-things-nautical. Your site can be long on the gifty knickknacks, but the recipients of your customers' gifts will appreciate it if you included some practical items like waterproof watches, navigational charts and maps, boat horns, and life jackets. You could also include appropriate clothing such as windbreakers, raingear, boat shoes, and various other practical items. Chances are if you want to start a site like this you are a sailor yourself. Even so, get a boating aficionado to help you find unusual and useful items for your online store—you'll get plenty of help if you offer them a generous discount on items they buy from you.

10. New Age

Crystals, incense, wall hangings, and books with new age approaches are great gift items to include on a website geared to the new ager. This movement has shown little slowdown. If it interests you, capture the new age mood in your website design and offer products that interest this group. Music, herbal remedies, yoga and meditation information and gear are all items you could offer. Check out other new age websites to be sure you are appealing to this group—which is probably a group you are familiar with and enjoy if you are going to start a business in this category.

11. Women/Men

A gift website geared specifically toward men or specifically toward women could go in many directions. Your biggest challenge is to avoid stereotypes. One idea for a women's website, for instance, is to sell women's work clothing—smaller sized work gloves, Timberland boots, Carhart coveralls and coats. The person looking for a gift for the outdoor woman would find it here.

For a man-specific site, you could offer unique items that are exclusively male such as ties and belts and hats. Women often find it difficult to buy gifts for men, so unique items in these classically male categories would be of interest to them. These websites are ones where you want to be sure to sell gift certificates for those afraid to choose.

12. Western

Like country, Western style is not going out of fashion soon. For the horse lover or rugged individual on a gift list, there are myriad products that would fit that bill.

13. Religious

Believers of almost all faiths are potential gift recipients of items appropriate to their faith. Your site could also include books and other practical items. You may want to limit your gift site to one particular religion or go for a more secular site offering items in many denominations.

14. Handcrafted

A gift website offering handcrafted gifts could go in almost any direction. Almost everyone appreciates the quality that handcrafted items usually offer. This product line could include just about anything, so you might do well to focus in one category, such as jewelry, clothing, or a specific handmade item such as candles or bookends. Again, this is a very fun product line to shop in! Be sure to get samples to inspect the quality of the items before offering them to your customers.

15. Home

Gifts for the home is a very popular category and has myriad options for items you can offer. Keep them small (i.e., you probably don't want to sell ovens or kitchen sinks) and manageable. Most people won't be buying huge items as gifts. But still stretch your imagination—outdoor garden décor, windchimes, handcrafted birdfeeders, unique ways to stash the remote control are all fun items to give as gifts.

16. Food

Food, glorious food is always a perfect gift! With overnight delivery you don't even have to avoid perishable foods. But things that keep are often best. People appreciate getting coffee, nuts, gourmet popcorn, tea, bread premixes, the list is endless. You can enhance your product line by offering kitchen appliances, wine glasses, cutting boards, or anything that relates to the food items you are selling.

17. Nature

Humans are in love with nature. Stretch your imagination—CDs with whale songs, birdfeeders, binoculars, field guides, warm hiking socks, all-natural bug repellent. Pick things that a gift giver looking for something for the nature lover on her list would look at and go "I never knew such a thing existed. How clever. Mal (or Louise) would love this!"

18. Seniors

The senior set are a gift category all their own. You can have some things that are strictly safety/senior oriented, but don't forget that seniors tend to have a lot of leisure time; carry unique items for activities they might want to pursue with their time. Again, you are looking for your customer to have that "aha!" moment where he sees something that he never knew existed but knows would be just perfect for that senior person on his gift list.

19. Toys

Almost everyone has to buy for kids here and there, and what more appropriate gift for kids than a toy! But have some fun looking for unique toys that are going to hold up to the wear and tear administered by a child. Be sure you are buying from safety-conscious manufacturers who are using lead-free paint and are aware of other hazards to avoid in kids' items. And don't just buy safety-conscious items, advertise the fact! This is a selling point that shouldn't be hidden in your "about you" section on your site. Have your website designer create and place a banner or starburst or other symbol that clearly indicates that your business sells products that have safety first in mind.

20. Corporate

Corporate gifts can represent lots of money in the gift-giving world. One way to approach this is to start with a line of gifts you like and then offer them to the corporate world. Or work with specific companies to create a gift line that they can choose from when they need corporate gifts to send to the hotel room of visiting clients or have as gifts to conference speakers. This is a creative and interesting gift category that is limited in possibilities only by your imagination.

Chapter 3

Day 2:
Focus on Inventory

*O*rdering inventory not only takes time, inventory also takes time for the items to reach you. On Day 2, you will focus on getting your products ordered and on their way to you. Here are the things you will accomplish on Day 2:

➡ Determine what companies will provide your opening inventory.

➡ Determine what you will order from them, making sure to stay within your opening inventory budget.

→ Place your orders.

→ Outline the final details of your warehouse location to be sure you are ready to receive your orders.

→ Make certain your warehousing area is set up to accommodate the items you have ordered and has space to store them.

Sources

As we mentioned in Chapter 1: Before Day 1, your inventory will come from myriad sources, including wholesalers, local crafters, importers, garage sales, and eBay. The sources are almost endless. How you deal with each one will be different. And what you can get from them for opening inventory will differ as well. Some will give you anything you want, others will control your inventory levels (particularly if they allow returns), others such as crafters who make all their items will have only a certain number of an item available for you to order anyway. You probably want to have a mix of these inventory sources.

How Much Do You Need to Sell?

Amateur entrepreneurs often overlook having enough to sell to meet their sales projections. This is where you go back to your business plan and pull out the pro forma financials you created. How much did you project in revenue for the first month of business? What do you need to sell to make that number?

Let's pretend you are opening an online site that sells astronomy-related items. This will include small-ticket items such as glow-in-the-dark stars and planets that you can put on your ceiling, medium-priced items such as the complete encyclopedia of the galaxy and astronomical maps, and big-ticket items such as telescopes. When you made your projections, you used these items to figure out how much you might be able to make in a month. Perhaps you estimated that you would sell 100 small-ticket items, 30 medium-priced items, and 1 telescope per month. In order to meet those projections, you need to have those items in stock at all times in order to sell them.

MARKETING SAVVY

If you need to sell one telescope per month in order to meet your sales projections, not only do you need to have that telescope in stock in order to sell it but you also need to figure out what kind of marketing you need to do in order to sell that telescope each month. Sales and marketing are intimately connected.

Replenishing Your Supply

Once you sell that telescope for the month, you need to immediately have another one on the way to sell the next month to keep up with your income projections (or to beat projections and sell two in one month!). Keeping up on your existing inventory and inventory needs is paramount. Having suppliers that are ready to ship you product immediately is also important.

Many suppliers require you order a certain amount to get a specified discount. For instance, if you order 1 or 2 copies of a single book, you get them at a 20 percent discount. If you order 3 to 5 copies, you get them at 30 percent off the cover price, 6 to 25 at 40 percent, 26 to 100 at 45 percent, and so on.

Your financial projections may be (and should be) based on getting a minimum of a 40 percent markup on everything you sell. This allows you to cover your operating costs. Anything less and you will need to trim the expenses side accordingly. So go ahead and order 6 to 25 copies of that book to get the 40 percent discount.

But think carefully before ordering 26 of something to get a 5 percent extra discount with the idea that more discount is always better. In some cases it may in fact be well worth it—your best-selling or "signature" item, for example, is one that you do, in fact, want to get the best discount for. You know you will sell 26 of them in three months, or whatever your necessary "turn" for that item is. But if the item is new to you or one that has been slow to turn, try it out with a smaller quantity and see how it goes before reaching for those higher discount points.

Returns

Returns from customers are one thing, but returning overstock to your suppliers is another. Some suppliers sell everything nonreturnable—if it doesn't sell, it's your job to find a way to get it out of your warehouse. Some suppliers do allow returns within a certain period. The book industry, for example, allows you to buy books on a returnable basis, but often with a lower purchase discount than the gift market supplier typically offers. Many also offer better terms if you buy nonreturnable.

Keep in mind, however, that although being able to return unsold stock sounds appealing, it is time consuming and costly (at least one direction of shipping, sometimes both, falls in your lap) to pack things back up and return them. You are responsible for their safe return, and the items must be in re-saleable condition. This is a lot of time that you could be spending actually selling something that gives you the 40 percent markup you need.

Don't fall into the trap of relying on returning items to pay your bill to that supplier. This would be a red flag that your business is floundering and needs attention somewhere else, like an increase in marketing to increase sales or trimming expenses.

Credit

It is unlikely you will be able to get immediate credit from suppliers, but this is something you want to work toward. Credit with suppliers means you can get inventory and, ideally, sell it before the invoice is due. Therefore, you are using your suppliers' money to stock your inventory and not paying out until you have money in hand.

Typically, suppliers require you to pay up front for your opening inventory. This can result in startup capital needs being relatively high. Once you establish an account and a relationship with a supplier, 30-day terms is common. It may put credit limits on your account, lower at first but increasing as your relationship grows.

Developing strong relationships with suppliers is critical to the success of your business. There may come a time when you have the possibility of making a large sale of a certain item; a supplier that you have a long and positive

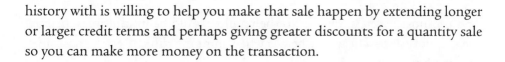

CLICK TIP

When ordering new products, always ask the supplier if there are digital product photos available for you to use. That way you have immediate shots to upload to your website and don't have to wait for product to arrive and set up a shoot yourself or hire and wait for someone you've hired to do it for you.

history with is willing to help you make that sale happen by extending longer or larger credit terms and perhaps giving greater discounts for a quantity sale so you can make more money on the transaction.

Drop Shipping

Having items "drop shipped" from the manufacturer can be a key method for controlling inventory, especially on large items. And it can be particularly useful for online retailers. For instance, if the astronomy gift site shows telescopes for sale on its website and a customer orders one, the e-tailer doesn't even need to have that, or any, telescope in stock—the order can be taken and the telescope drop shipped directly from the manufacturer's warehouse to the customer.

This saves in many areas for the e-tailer:

- paying up front for inventory to sit in the warehouse
- cost of packing materials, especially for specialty items like telescopes
- the cost of having someone pack up the item and get it shipped out
- space in the warehouse
- the possibility the item gets damaged while in the warehouse

The manufacturer doesn't always assume complete responsibility here. There is often an extra drop-ship charge from the manufacturer to the retailer (e-tail or brick-and-mortar) to cover some of the costs that the e-tailer would have normally incurred. For example, even though the manufacturer would have had to send the item to the e-tailer to sell opposed to shipping it to the customer, the manufacturer often charges the customer for that shipping.

CLICK TIP

With drop shipping, you may risk giving up your customer to the manufacturer if the manufacturer sells to individuals. Even though a customer is unlikely to buy multiple telescopes, the manufacturer may sell maps, lenses, and related products that could take from your business with that customer. And at the very least, they get to market to the customer in a way that you don't.

And for most items, shipment to the retailer would be in multiples, making the shipping costs cheaper, whereas when shipping directly to the customer, just one item is shipped.

For the most part, the item in question dictates whether drop shipping is cost effective or not. Shipping a box full of smaller items to you for you to sort out and ship to individual customers can be more cost effective for the manufacturer. But shipping one large item directly to the consumer can be cost effective for everyone.

Turnover

Inventory requirements for online businesses are not much different from those for brick-and-mortar stores. In fact, if anything, you need to keep a closer eye on inventory because your website is marketing your products to the entire internet customer base, not just to the local people who come into your store.

Turnover determines how often you need to order to replenish your inventory. Turnover is stated using a predetermined turn rate, perhaps items sold in a month or even a year. The more "turns" an item has, the better the income on that item. Be careful not to get burned on an item, however. Keep tabs on trends. For instance, perhaps a book you've had five copies of in stock for two months suddenly sells out in one day. So you order eight more. Two sell that week, and the other six are sitting there two months later. Sudden interest in a book typically has to do with a review or author appearance on a television show or some other publicity that gives a quick burst in sales. Don't get burned buying additional inventory based on that short-term burst! Books are usually returnable but returning inventory is expensive. It helps if suppliers can keep you posted when they know one of their products is going to get some publicity.

Calculate Your Costs

The ideal formula for a successful online gift business is to be able to purchase or acquire your inventory for a low cost per unit and then resell that inventory at the highest retail price possible in order to generate the maximum profit. No matter what quantity you're buying, always know what your cost-per-unit is, and make sure there's enough profit margin to cover all of your operating expenses (including, for example, your own salary, the cost of operating your website, and your company's marketing/advertising). You probably won't figure out exactly what that figure is per item, but you can figure out an overall percentage that is the minimum discount you can accept and still cover your expenses.

Be sure to calculate appropriate shipping charges, sales taxes (if applicable), order processing fees, warehousing costs, packaging costs, insurance, finance charges (interest), and any other expenses that diminish your profit margins.

You'll quickly discover that in most cases when acquiring inventory, you receive the best discounts when you buy in quantity. Depending on the product, this might mean ordering dozens, hundreds, or even thousands of the same product at once in order to benefit from the savings offered by a manufacturer,

---

CLICK TIP

If you're maintaining any inventory in your home, your office, or an outside facility, you need to have insurance to protect this investment. Check with your insurer, but it is unlikely your homeowner's insurance will cover business-related inventory or equipment against theft or damage.

wholesaler, or distributor. Don't be completely snowed by this supposed "savings" though. Keep in mind that when placing larger orders, there are some hidden costs—e.g., shipping and warehousing—that you need to account for. Be prepared to crunch some numbers to determine what's best for your business.

If you use credit to acquire your inventory and you don't pay the bill when it is due, you will also need to calculate interest into your per unit pricing.

Storage

You have decided what to order, and the shipments are coming in fast and furious. Your storage needs are going to depend a lot on what you are selling. Of course, there is always size to consider. But you also need to consider whether your products need a climate-controlled environment, refrigeration in the case of foodstuffs, or require that they be stored flat or rolled or standing up or laying down—all the idiosyncracies that come with unique products.

And your gift market may be mixed. If the category of your online gift store is gardening, the ceramic pots you sell can be set on a shelf in almost any climate—cold, hot, humid, dry, it isn't really going to affect the ceramic. However, you may also sell live plants. These must be stored in an area that gives them the right temperature to keep them alive and healthy. And they may need to be in a space where they can be watered without damaging the storage area or other products.

Another key storage consideration is making sure that your fast-moving products are readily accessible. If you sell 50 small widgets a day and you have to rummage through and crawl around a supply of mammoth products that you sell one of a week in a good week, you are wasting time. Not to mention you will be frustrated and the mammoth product in the way may be subjected to unnecessary wear and tear.

Racking

You don't want to spend a lot of money initially on racking systems. But if you are selling a product that needs special care, it would probably be best to invest in proper storage racking. Unlike a brick-and-mortar store, you won't need to consider visibility and display appeal to customers. But products can quickly become "shopworn" without proper storage. Sending out tired-looking product costs money in the long run—products will be returned, customers will be unhappy with their orders, and you will lose repeat business. It's better to spend the money up front for appropriate storage; although it's impossible to track, you can be sure the investment will quickly pay for itself.

Receiving

Most of your incoming shipments need to have someone around to receive them. You must figure out who that is going to be. If your online gift business is a full-time venture that you are setting up completely in your home—from the computer you control your website with to the area you pick, pack, and ship out orders—then this is easily resolved. The person receiving the inventory is you. You're already there either because you are home or because you are working on your business.

Of course, this doesn't mean that you can never leave your house! You will get to know the timing of your couriers and can be around when they come. And you can create a safe, dry place for shipments that don't need signatures to be left when you are not at home.

The point is that you can't open a warehouse space and have no one ever there to receive shipments. If couriers leave shipments at your home when you are not there, you will presumably be coming home in a reasonable amount of time to take care of those shipments. But if you maintain an independent warehouse, your shipments will sit on the loading dock or outside the door until the next time you show up at the warehouse.

Another option is to have a warehouse space that also houses your office. This way you are working on your website in your office at your warehouse and are around during the day when shipments come.

Your website gift business may be a part-time venture while you hold down a full-time job, which means no one is ever around to receive your shipments. If you are receiving inventory at home and your home is in an area where shipments are safe until you get there, this can be fine. Many gift businesses, however, contain at least a couple items that are very valuable such as diamond-encrusted watches or custom jewelry. It is best not to leave them sitting out on the sidewalk, and they also may require a signature from the courier. Perhaps your work environment is such that these shipments can be delivered to your work address, which can be fine if these shipments happen only once a month or so. But if you need to have shipments sent to your work address a couple times a week, the shipments may not be so acceptable.

Another warehousing option that can help solve delivery problems is leasing space within an operating warehouse. Many warehouses are already over capacity and wouldn't be able to do this. But some may have a few rows of shelving in a remote corner that could be the perfect place for your business to operate out of. While you will still need to purchase a certain quantity of supplies—appropriate cartons, packing materials, and the like—in this situation you may have access to a pallet jack, pallets, and other equipment and large items that you don't need very often or very much of. This access to equipment can be convenient and helpful in reducing expenses.

The other convenience to this arrangement is that, depending on how your lease is structured, your shipments can be received during the day by the receivers who are already working in the warehouse. They can collect the products and move them to your area once a day.

You will, in this situation, need to be able to get into the warehouse in its off hours—although some warehouses operate 24 hours a day, making access a nonissue. You need to be comfortable being there by yourself during the off hours.

This can be a perfect arrangement but the key is to be sure to outline every detail in a contract.

- ➡ What supplies you need to take care of yourself and what is provided by the leasor, such as pallets, pallet jacks, pallet wrap.
- ➡ What services the leasor provides in the contract, such as shipping and receiving, bringing your shipments to your area in the warehouse, trash pickup, electricity for a space heater, computer, internet services, and phone service.
- ➡ What you are and are not allowed to do—move shelving? Add shelving? Post signage? Paint?

➡ Are you allowed to use facilities such as the bathroom, kitchen, microwave, refrigerator, or snack machine?

➡ Are you allowed to hire someone to work in your area? If so, does the warehouse manager need to be involved with that hiring, such as security clearances?

Some of these details vary depending on the type of gift business you have. But it can't be emphasized enough that this warehouse-sharing arrangement can be a perfect solution. You just need to be sure to outline every detail.

Sales and Closeouts

At some point, you will want to cut your losses and sell overstocked inventory at a discount. Retail stores are great at this, and online stores can be, too. Be sure to alert your customer list to any inventory clearing. Carrying those poor sellers is usually more expensive than blowing them out at a lower price.

Keep in mind that the lower your profit margin is on a product, the less that item contributes to your bottom line. So don't do this willy nilly. Devise a strategy that helps you determine when it is time to put a product on clearance—pick a landmark that makes the decision for you. For instance, not one of that item has sold in 30 days. Or the sales level decreases by 70 percent. Or the item is on the verge of not being able to be returned to the manufacturer for credit.

Then mark it down. Mark it down substantially, not in tiny increments. If you really want to move something, you have to make it initially so appealing to customers that they buy it at this fantastic discount for fear that if they don't decide soon it will be sold out at such a great price.

Cash Flow

Inventory contributes greatly to cash flow issues. Your inventory purchases and sales of that inventory are where your main revenue and expenses come from. If you have a large supply of inventory hanging around but need to pay for it before you sell it, cash flow can become a big issue.

Dealing with the Rushes and the Slow Times

In the gift business, you will most likely find the Christmas holiday season to be your busiest season. It can be difficult when the majority of your sales come at the very end of the year. In the very short window between Thanksgiving and Christmas, your business can look very different from what the year so far has brought.

Some gift businesses aren't quite as holiday-focused as others. Yours may be a business with gifts that are more appropriate as bridal presents—and therefore June and September are your busiest months. Or perhaps Valentine's Day is the busiest holiday for your gifts. You need to consider this seasonal factor in your budgeting and revenue projections so that your financials don't look wrong because you haven't accounted for this seasonal issue.

For a business in which a lot of transactions are condensed into a short time, you may also need to hire help. It is still vitally important that orders get out the door promptly—even more so during a time like Christmas when the couriers and postal service are backed up themselves. Be sure to factor in a part-time seasonal position or two when calculating your expenses.

What to Carry

How do you know what to stock in your online gift store? This is another area where your well-crafted business plan comes in handy. The key to knowing what to carry for products is in understanding the focus of your business.

If you are aiming to be a provider of gifts to the wealthy consumer, no matter what the actual product line you decide on, you need to offer products that carry brand names that will impress the buyer's gift recipient. This holds true of tools, equine apparel, or handbags. For this clientele you need to be sure to search for things that are not available at Walmart or Target.

The other end of the spectrum is the shopper looking for gifts at discount prices. Brand names are not an issue, although brand name rip-offs may be appealing.

Your category makes a difference. For example, Karen Campbell with her Campbell's Scotties (who is interviewed later in this book) can carry anything that has a Scottie dog on it. However, as she has come to learn more about Scotties over the years, Karen has also become much more discerning in her choices—the dogs shown on the products she buys must be true representatives of the breed. And her customers have come to expect that of the items she offers on her site.

Once again, a practical matter is to keep stocking and shipping in mind. Even if Karen finds a dog crate with a Scottie emblazoned on, it doesn't mean she wants to sell it on her site—it could mean storage, packing, and shipping issues she doesn't want to deal with. Or alternatively, it might just mean finding out if the manufacturer offers drop shipping or at least packaging that makes the item ready to ship without having to repack.

Chances are your online gift business will have a theme. Or maybe it has many themes. You can start your inventory building by focusing on one of your themes and building that category. Be careful about being quickly pigeonholed in one category, however, if you plan to expand your offerings.

Fulfilling Orders

As your advertising and marketing efforts begin to work and orders start to trickle in, it is time to start fulfilling orders, handling customer service issues, managing the bookkeeping tasks associated with running a business, maintaining inventory, and taking care of the many other order-related responsibilities required to run a retail business.

Customer service matters are covered fully in Day 7. But in the meantime, know your new customers care deeply about receiving correctly fulfilled orders in a very timely manner.

Order In, Ship Out

When an order comes in, you need to ship it out as soon as possible. In any business these days, but especially in the online world, customers expect fast turnaround. As soon as someone places an order, she'll be expecting it to be fulfilled and shipped quickly—and if she's opted to pay for rush shipping, there needs to be no delay. To accommodate the demands of your customers, you need to establish order fulfillment procedures and a "shipping department" that maintains all of the inventory and shipping supplies needed to get all new orders quickly processed and shipped out.

As mentioned before, for each product you decide to sell, you need to maintain an ample supply of appropriately sized boxes, padded envelopes, stuffing, packing tape, labels, and other shipping materials. Figure out exactly what you need and have a constant supply on hand. If there is no local outlet where you can readily purchase needed shipping supplies, you need a greater supply on hand. It is completely unnecessary for an order not to ship out because you don't have the proper packing materials.

Shipping Options

You need to decide what shipping options to extend to your customers. Options include the USPS, UPS, FedEx, and/or other shipping services in order to provide the following basic shipping options:

- Economy (five to seven days)
- Three-day
- Two-day
- Overnight

As an incentive to customers, some online business operators offer free economy (UPS/FedEx) or Priority Mail shipping (via the post office) and build these costs into the price of the product. When shipping is not built in, your website's shopping cart module needs to calculate shipping charges and add them to the customer's order total.

If you opt to ship your products via Priority Mail or Express Mail from the USPS, free envelopes and boxes are available. Based on the size of your product, you may also qualify for a flat shipping rate. For details about postage rates and to order free shipping supplies from the USPS, visit usps.com or your local post office branch.

To avoid daily trips to the local post office to buy stamps/postage and drop off packages, you can arrange for daily pick-up with your mail carrier but each package will need to have the proper postage already affixed. Thus, you might opt to acquire or rent a postage meter from a company like Pitney

Bowes (pitneybowes.com). Several models are available, based on the amount of shipping you'll be doing.

For a startup business looking to generate postage stamps in-house for shipping, Endicia offers complete, low-cost postage solutions that allow any computer connected to the internet to purchase and print postage using any type of printer, including DYMO label printers (sold separately, starting under $200 at dymostamps.com). Endicia postage solutions are available for PC or Mac computers. Although the required software is free of charge and can be downloaded from the company's website (endicia.com), there is a monthly fee of $15.95 to maintain an account, plus the cost of whatever U.S. postage you purchase.

Accounts with Shippers

You'll probably need to open accounts with the basic shippers—FedEx and/or UPS (and perhaps other couriers as well). Opening accounts with these companies takes just minutes and can be done online by visiting their websites (fedex.com and ups.com). You can also order free shipping supplies (envelopes, labels, and boxes) from each company's website. They will be delivered right to your door. When opening an account, you typically need a major credit card.

The prices these companies charge to ship your packages are based on several criteria, including the quantity of packages you ship on an ongoing basis (volume discounts apply), the shipping services you use, the size and weight of each package, your geographic location, and the destination of each package. To save money, you want to compare rates among these popular couriers. In many situations, the prices quoted to ship an identical package are vastly

---

CLICK TIP

To quickly compare shipping rates among the couriers, visit iship.com/priceit/price.asp, redroller.com/shippingcenter/home, or pakmail.com/estimator.

CLICK TIP

Requiring that the recipient sign for the package upon receipt can eliminate confusion when a customer doesn't receive her order in a timely manner. However, requiring a signature can also be inconvenient for the customer since many customers will not be home when the package arrives. Use common sense to decide—perhaps only your most expensive items require a signature. Indicate this on the order form and perhaps have a box that the customer can check indicating they declined the signature option and let them take on the responsibility.

different. You can also save money by dropping off your packages at a FedEx or UPS location rather than scheduling a pick-up.

Some products may be more cost effective via one shipper over another. Check rates on all of your common products and especially on any products that are delicate, extra large, or extra heavy. There can be quite a difference among the shippers depending on what their specialty is.

Depending on what you're shipping, you may also need to purchase insurance for each package (at additional cost). Don't forget to budget in all these shipping-related charges, including the cost of items like packing tape, stuffing, and labels, and pass these costs along to your customer by building them into the price of the product you're selling.

Packing

Shipping items means that they need to be packed before they can be shipped. Some packaging items you need to have on hand include

- cartons of the appropriate size and strength for your products, but also for multiple products to go in one carton.
- padding of whatever kind you choose—bubble wrap, shredded paper, packing peanuts, crunched cardboard.
- sealing tape.
- labels that can be printed from your computer.
- packing slips that can be printed from your computer.

As you pack up orders and prepare them for shipping, make sure to include ample padding or stuffing to ensure your product arrives at its destination undamaged. When developing the shipping policies and procedures for your company, you also need to determine what will be included in the packaging with each order. Some possibilities include

- ➡ a printed invoice,
- ➡ a customer feedback card,
- ➡ a printed catalog,
- ➡ a personalized "Thank You for Your Order" letter,
- ➡ printed directions for returning or exchanging the product,
- ➡ special money-saving offers for repeat customers, and/or
- ➡ coupons to entice customers to visit and order again.

Besides these materials, you need to create standard packaging instructions for anyone who is doing packing and shipping for you (and even for yourself so you can be consistent each time!). If you hire someone, even your mom, to pack and ship your orders, that person needs to know that the handmade glass suncatcher should be wrapped in the extra-large bubble wrap and placed in its own sturdy cardboard box even if it is to be shipped with other items inside a larger package.

Also, from a record-keeping standpoint, you need to keep detailed records of your customers and related shipping and order details. If you choose one of the e-commerce turnkey solutions, these tools may be provided. Otherwise, you need to acquire third-party software, such as ACT! (act.com), QuickBooks

---

CLICK TIP

Box manufacturers can help you decide what kind of box to use for shipping each of your products. They know the test strength of each of the cardboard products they offer and how much weight the package will hold. They also have other specialty packaging like double-wall boxes for special items. Use your suppliers to help you make decisions when they know more than you do.

CLICK TIP

Even if your business's shipping department is a small table in your home with shipping supplies stored underneath, automate the process so you can save time, be consistent, and maintain accurate records.

(insuit.com), or FileMaker Pro (filemaker.com) to help you manage these important tasks.

It's essential that you be able to quickly track any orders you've shipped, so having the applicable customer and shipping information at your disposal is important. Have contingency plans in place to deal with a wide range of potential scenarios and problems, including:

- An order arrives to its destination damaged.
- An order gets delayed being shipped out.
- An order gets lost in transit.
- The customer wishes to cancel or change his order before it gets processed.
- The customer wants to return the product.
- The customer wants to exchange the product.
- The order was incorrectly fulfilled.

Dealing with these and other issues, which will no doubt arise, requires you to interact directly with your customers as well as with the shipping company you used. Remember, regardless of the situation, always strive to provide prompt, courteous, and highly professional customer service. Your goal should be to quickly transform any potentially negative situation into a positive one (from your customer's perspective) in order to retain him as a valued customer, generate repeat business, and increase your chances of benefitting from positive word-of-mouth advertising.

Inventory Care

The fact that you are an online business doesn't eliminate some of the good old-fashioned retail concerns. One is that it is important to keep your inventory in

CATALOG ALTERNATIVE

You may want to include a printed catalog in your shipments. If printing a full catalog seems too expensive, think smaller. You can print a small four-page flier showcasing your most popular items, items on sale, or whatever you want to promote during that period.

perfect condition. As mentioned earlier, having appropriate storage, especially for those items that are unusual in size, shape, or material, is critical to sending out quality products to your customers. Keep your storage area clean and dust-free. Make sure any employees or other help you have know that smoking and eating in inventory areas is completely unacceptable.

Taxes

Be sure you and your tax accountant know the tax laws in your state regarding inventory. Inventory is subject to taxes, and it is critical you pay attention to the potential costs of carrying excess inventory.

In Conclusion

Inventory is a critical component of any business. Don't be duped into thinking that it isn't also a huge component of an online business as well. Doing business in cyberspace also includes physical products that need to be stored and shipped. Inventory is a significant issue for any retail business and needs to be carefully considered.

Chapter 4

Day 3:
Turnkey Startups
for E-Tailing

*T*o get your e-tail business up and running in a week and capitalize on those $144 billion in online sales expected to hit by 2010, you need to consider a turnkey operation. These solutions can get you going at an initial investment of as little as several hundred dollars. You don't have to hire a team of programmers to design and launch a website from scratch (which, in any case, would take weeks or months to create and cost you thousands, if not tens of thousands of dollars in development costs). With an e-commerce turnkey solution, you choose from a selection of professional-looking website templates that you can fully customize to suit your specific online business.

Each template includes the components needed to create a highly functional e-commerce website capable of handling secure transactions. In addition, there are other cost- and time-savings aspects such as website hosting services and the ability to accept major credit cards and other online payment options. These entail an additional fee but save you in other ways, such as not having to acquire a separate merchant account.

Sure, the website templates may not offer all of the flashy design elements you might like to incorporate into your site, but they do offer the core functionality necessary to launch your e-commerce business and to test its viability. Once your business is successful, you should definitely plan on expanding and fine-tuning the website on an ongoing basis.

In this chapter, you will learn about turnkey operations:

- ➡ How to you pick the right turnkey solution for your business.
- ➡ Who are the main turnkey solution providers currently on the market.
- ➡ How to recognize when you have outgrown your turnkey website.

The Good, the Bad, and the Ugly of Using Turnkey Solutions

OK, the title of this book includes "in a week." Realistically, therefore, the main reason to go with an e-commerce turnkey solution to launch your online gift business is time you'll save. Many of the companies that offer these turnkey solutions have created an entire suite of easy-to-use online tools to assist you in designing, creating, launching, and then managing your business.

Unless you really want to be in website design, why do this all yourself when these templates can take care of the essentials for you? In addition, you do not need to do or know any programming; it is all done for you. And there are so many options that you can still customize your site and have it look almost completely unique. Money is also a key factor in using a web template. The startup costs are considerably lower than if you were to design a site from scratch.

Although each company offers a different selection, many include modules for maintaining a customer database, managing inventory, and keeping detailed order shipment records (including the ability to print shipping labels and track packages shipped via the U.S. Postal Service, FedEx, or UPS). Usually several different e-commerce turnkey solution options are available from each company. Each package comes with a slightly different selection of tools and resources at different price points, so you don't have to overspend in order to launch your business.

For example, GoDaddy.com is a well-established company that offers a vast selection of easy-to-use online tools and resources designed to make creating and launching an e-commerce website fast and easy. If you'll be initially selling no more than 20 different products, Go Daddy's Quick Shopping Cart Economy Edition ($6.99 to $9.99 per month) offers the tools you need to create an online store showcasing up to 20 products. You'll also be able to accept PayPal an as online payment method.

GoDaddy.com's Quick Shopping Cart Deluxe Edition ($20.99 to $29.99 per month) lets you expand from there, offering additional website creation tools and features, including the ability to showcase and sell up to 100 products from your site. The Quick Shopping Cart Premium Edition ($34.99 to $49.99 per month) allows you to showcase and sell an unlimited number of products.

Website hosting and online security (including the ability to create an SSL-enabled site) is included with each Quick Shopping Cart package. (You'll learn more about specific packages in the roundup at the end of this chapter.)

The eBay Stores (stores.ebay.com) and eBay ProStores (prostores.com) sites offer distinct business models and several different service tiers or packages for online merchants. Each of these packages comes with the tools to build your store using templates that can be customized in hundreds of ways. The tools to promote your store, manage sales, and track your success are also included.

The various turnkey based solutions are ideal for startup businesses. However, as your online gift business grows, you may want to add website functionality that is not available from the e-commerce turnkey solution

---

CLICK TIP

Whether you are creating a website from scratch or using a turnkey solution template, spend time looking at other websites that you think are well designed and that you'd like yours to emulate. Unlike when you did this for your competitive research, these sites do not have to be online gift sites. Sticking to retail sites is probably most logical, but any retail site, gift or not, can showcase features, functionality, and design elements you are likely to want to incorporate into your site. Don't forget to get out your crystal ball and think about what your needs might be in the future. All of this helps you choose a turnkey solution that's best suited for your business venture.

---

provider you chose. Thus, as you shop around for a service provider, look for one that allows you to expand and grow your website over time so you can add functionality as it becomes necessary.

One of the big drawbacks many turnkey solutions have is that the design capabilities and functionality you are able to offer on your site are limited by what's offered by the turnkey solution provider you opt to deal with. For example, you may be limited by how much you can actually customize a template in terms of its look or functionality. For a simple online gift operation, this should not pose a problem at all. However, be aware that at some point down the road, you may outgrow what the service provider is capable of offering.

At that point, you will find it necessary to investigate different options. Here is where you might be ready to have a custom website created from scratch. Or perhaps you decide on an interim solution and hire your own programmers to further customize the website template you're utilizing.

Reducing Startup Costs

In the past, creating and hosting a secure website capable of handling online financial transactions (processing credit card orders, for example) was usually the most costly aspect of launching an online business. Today, thanks to the turnkey solutions discussed in this chapter, it has become an inexpensive and straightforward process.

As you calculate your startup budget, you want to allocate as much money as possible for designing and launching the most professional and easy-to-use website possible, as well as for properly marketing the site in order to generate traffic to it. Simply publishing a website on the internet and registering it with the search engines and web directories, such as Google and Yahoo!, is not enough. It is, however, an important start, as you'll discover in Day 5: Marketing.

Selecting the Right E-Commerce Turnkey Solution

Every online business has different needs, based on what's being sold, to whom products are being sold, and what features and functionality the online merchant wishes to incorporate into her e-commerce site. Once you pinpoint what you want and need, finding a complete turnkey solution that meets your requirements at a price you can afford is a relatively straightforward process.

As you look at what each e-commerce turnkey solution offers, don't just look at a list of features and make your decision. Be sure to visit several e-commerce websites that currently use the services of the company you're thinking about working with, and invest time exploring those websites. Considering

---

CLICK TIP

In addition to the core functionality you need to operate your e-commerce website, some turnkey solutions offer the ability to automatically or easily list your items for sale through online auction sites, such as eBay.com. For startup online entrepreneurs, offering products on eBay.com, for example, can be a way to promote a new business, test market new products, and generate additional revenue. If your turnkey solution provider offers an eBay listing tool, for example, this could save you time and effort listing and managing online auctions for your products. Likewise, if you plan to use QuickBooks to manage your business's finances, seamless integration between your turnkey solution and this software is beneficial.

---

how your own site will be customized, do the sites you're looking at offer the professional look, functionality, and user interface that could work well for your business? Will you be able to easily customize the templates to create a site you're proud of and that meets your needs? Ultimately, choosing the best turnkey solution to meet the needs of your unique online business could mean the difference between success and failure.

CLICK TIP

Listing your products on services such as Google Product Search (google.com/base/help/sellongoogle.html) and/or price comparison websites, such as Nextag.com (merchants.nextag.com/serv/main/advertise/ Advertise.do) can also be useful marketing tools. Google AdWords, Yahoo Small Business, and Microsoft adCenter are also services that can be used to promote your business. Some turnkey solutions make using these services to promote your products a seamless process that ties directly to the management tools used to operate your e-tail website.

Round-Up

As we've discussed so far, using a complete e-tail turnkey solution to design, launch, and operate your online business offers a wide range of benefits:

- No programming is required.
- Startup costs are very low.
- Your site can be designed and launched in less than one week.
- Using a template provided by the turnkey solution provider, it's easy to make your site look professional and offer the functionality required to make it easy to use for your visitors.
- The turnkey solution providers offer all of the tools needed to design, launch, and operate your online business for one monthly fee.

This chapter provides details about some of the most popular complete e-commerce turnkey solutions available from well-known providers, such as eBay.com, GoDaddy.com, Network Solutions, and Yahoo! The companies and the products described here, however, are only a small sampling of the turnkey solutions available to startup online business owners. Search around the internet and also look at what other sites are using.

Shopping for Your E-Commerce Turnkey Solution

As you finalize your online gift business and determine what you require from your site, you want to look closely at the turnkey offerings to find a solution that's best suited to your business concept. In addition to comparing the startup costs and ongoing monthly fees associated with each service, you want to evaluate the tools and resources offered by the service provider. They might include

- professional quality and selection of the site templates being offered.
- ease of use of the website design tools and other resources offered to help operate your business.
- technical support services provided.
- e-commerce functions that can be easily incorporated into your website using the development tools provided.
- ability to accept and process online payments from customers.
- online security measures your site will be able to incorporate.
- resources offered to help you market and promote your online business.
- ability to integrate easily your site's order and customer data with your accounting, spreadsheet, and/or order management software.
- ease of use, functionality, and professional appearance of the shopping cart module that will be incorporated into your site using the turnkey solution you select.
- extra fees or hidden charges you'll be responsible for in order to get your website designed, launched, and operational.
- expandability of your site in the future, using compatible third-party tools and resources.

Think through all of these points. Then when you know exactly what you are looking for from a turnkey solution, you can consider the other options discussed in the remainder of this chapter. Features and functionality, competitive pricing, and well-established, highly reputable service providers are all factors in the solutions discussed below.

CLICK TIP

To find additional companies offering similar solutions use an internet search engine such as Yahoo! or Google, and enter a search phrase such as, "e-commerce turnkey solution," "e-commerce solutions," "website creation solutions," or "web store development."

eBay Stores

Service provider: eBay.com

Website: pages.ebay.com/storefronts/start.html

Turnkey solution pricing: $15.95 to $299.95 per month

The folks at the online auction site, eBay have devised a way for sellers to take full advantage of the eBay auction sales model and also sell their products online using more traditional fixed-price methods. The result is eBay Stores (not to be confused with eBay ProStores, which are described later in the chapter).

For merchants, monthly fees start at $15.95 for a Basic Store, $49.95 for a Premium Store, or $299.95 for an Anchor Store. Once you choose which tier is most suitable for your needs as an online seller, you're provided with a roster of online tools to help you design and manage your store. In addition to these recurring monthly charges, eBay Stores also charges its merchants listing fees.

If you want to create an extremely professional online presence but don't have the experience or expertise to do this, eBay will put you in contact with a Certified eBay Stores Designer, who for an additional fee will help you design and launch your eBay Store. However, using eBay's Quick Store Set-Up module, you can customize a template and have a basic store up and running within a few hours.

Using a template, you can add your company's logo and store description; incorporate product photos for what you'll be selling and corresponding text-based product descriptions; divide your products into categories to make them easy to find; add a navigational toolbar to your main page; showcase specific products, sales, or promotions on your main page; plus add a variety of other features designed to make your customers' shopping experience efficient and your store a welcoming place to visit.

In fact, using one of the eBay Stores templates, you can customize up to 300 different elements of each template in order to create a unique shopping experience for your customers. Once your online store is designed and launched, the eBay Stores turnkey solution offers a variety of tools to help you market and promote your business and drive traffic to your site.

If you plan to get started selling between 10 and 49 items and expect to generate at least $100 in sales per month, the Basic Store is the perfect entry-level option. If you plan to sell more than 50 different products and/or generate at least $500 per month in sales, the Premium Store package is probably more suitable. The Anchor Store option is most suited to high-volume merchants looking for the maximum amount of exposure.

Because eBay Stores uses the online auction model, additional product listing fees apply. You do, however, save money on your listing fees as an eBay Stores operator compared to an individual posting single items. As an eBay Stores operator, you're also responsible for other fees, based on the tools and resources you use to promote and operate your store and the eBay Stores tier you sign up for.

To preview what an eBay Store can look like and see some of the functionality that can be built into an online business using this particular turnkey solution, visit the eBay Stores Design Center (pages.ebay.com/store fronts/designcenter.html). You can learn strategies for success using this turnkey solution from the free online eBay Stores Tutorials (pages.ebay.com/ storefronts/tutorials.html) and read success stories from fellow online merchants who currently use eBay Stores (pages.ebay.com/storefronts/success.html).

If your online business can benefit from customers being able to click on Buy It Now in order to immediately purchase your products at the fixed price points you set and you'd also like to sell your products by making them available through online auctions, the eBay Stores complete turnkey solution may be suitable for your online business.

According to eBay, within the eBay environment where millions of online auctions take place every day, eBay Stores offers, "a comprehensive e-commerce solution that helps you get more out of eBay's access to millions of shoppers worldwide. By showcasing all of your merchandise in one central location, an eBay Store creates a shopping destination where buyers can learn more about you, your products and your policies."

Furthermore, eBay reports that, "75 percent of eBay Stores sellers surveyed said that opening an eBay Store increased their sales. eBay Stores makes sellers successful by providing powerful tools to help sellers build, manage, promote, and track their eBay presence. We have found that higher volume and more experienced sellers who are committed to growing their sales and expect to have a part-time or full-time business on eBay tend to get the best results from their eBay Stores."

To open an eBay Store, you must have an active eBay account with a Feedback score of 20 or higher. You must also have your ID verified by eBay and have a PayPal account in good standing. The majority of your financial transactions related to your online sales generated will be handled through PayPal. This allows customers who have a PayPal account to make purchases using a major credit card, debit card, or electronic check, or transfer funds held in their pre-existing PayPal account.

The eBay Stores turnkey solution offers a comprehensive collection of tools to create, launch, and manage an online business, and takes full advantage of eBay's online auctions business model. It may or may not be suitable for your particular business venture, based on your unique goals and objectives.

eBay ProStores

Service provider: eBay.com

Phone number: (866) 747-3229

Website: prostores.com

Turnkey solution pricing: $6.95 to $249.95 per month, plus additional fees

Unlike eBay Stores, which uses the online auction model to allow merchants to sell their products, eBay's ProStores offers a complete solution for operating a more traditional e-commerce website, complete with Shopping Cart module.

As a complete solution, ProStores provides tools to handle everything from website development to inventory management and merchandising. For people first getting started and looking to test their online business idea, the ProStores Express service starts at just $6.95 per month, and it also charges a 1.5 percent per transaction fee on every sale. The Express service allows you to design a basic e-commerce website and get it up and running within a few hours, provided you'll be selling fewer than ten products.

For online business operators with more advanced and extensive needs, eBay offers ProStores Business, ProStores Advanced, and ProStores Enterprise ($29.95, $74.95, and $249.95 per month respectively, with a $.50 per transaction fee). With these different plans, online businesses can grow almost limitlessly as needed.

ProStores works seamlessly with eBay Stores and traditional eBay auctions, so merchants can also take advantage of online auctions to sell products. However, the goal of ProStores, like Yahoo! Stores (described later in the chapter), is to provide all the tools an online business operator needs, without requiring them to have any programming or website design skills or experience. All websites are created by fully customizing templates. ProStores, however, offers extreme flexibility when it comes to utilizing these templates, so if you do have programming skills (or wish to hire a programmer to modify your site), it's certainly possible.

If your website design needs exceed the capability that the online tools are capable of, ProStores offers a team of professional website designers who for an additional fee can create e-commerce sites from scratch or add full customization to existing templates. A fully functional e-commerce site can be created for a one-time fee of $399 to $649, depending on the site development package you purchase.

For example, the $649 website design package utilizes all of ProStore's capabilities and includes a customized version of the following web pages: Homepage, About Us, Customer Service, Store Location(s), Privacy Policy, FAQs, Store Policies, an online catalog featuring up to 20 products (adding additional products costs $20 each or you can do it yourself for free), a fully integrated shopping cart module, plus PayPal and/or online credit card processing functionality (with basic shipping and sales tax calculations). For an additional fee, ProStores will even maintain your site and keep it updated with new content that you provide.

Of course, if you don't wish to use ProStores professionals to design and maintain your website, you can use the online tools provided to do everything yourself or hire your own team of freelance professionals.

According to eBay, "ProStores offers a fully-featured Web store that can be customized specifically for each online seller. Unlike an eBay Store, ProStores sites are accessed through a URL unique to the seller and have no eBay branding. ProStores sellers are also responsible for driving their own traffic. While items on ProStores sites will sell at fixed prices only, they can also be easily listed onto the eBay Marketplace in either the auction or fixed price formats."

ProStores Business and service tiers above are fully integrated with many popular online payment gateways and merchant account providers, which means no additional software is required for your online store to accept and process credit card payments with your own merchant account. Some of the merchant account providers ProStores is fully compatible with include: Authorize.net (authorize.net), CyberSource (cybersource.com), Innovative Gateway Solutions (innovativegateway.com), LinkPoint (linkpoint.com), Payflow Pro (paypal.com), and QuickBooks Merchant Services (quickbooks merchantservice.com).

From a bookkeeping and client database management standpoint, ProStores is compatible with several third-party software packages, including QuickBooks from Intuit (quickbooks.com). A variety of online marketing, advertising, and promotional tools is also available.

For startup online businesses and business operators first learning about e-commerce, ProStores offers technical support, easy-to-use tutorials, and a comprehensive set of online tools to handle virtually all aspects of getting your business venture designed, launched, and fully operational. This turnkey solution is ideal for people with little or no programming knowledge. To see several fully operational e-commerce websites that use eBay ProStores, visit prostores.com/prostores-featured.shtml.

FatCow.com

Service provider: FatCow

Phone number: (866) 544-9343

Website: fatcow.com

Turnkey solution pricing: $29.95 to $49.95 per month, plus additional fees

Virtually every internet service provider (ISP) in the world offering website hosting also offers tools to its customers for creating and launching an e-commerce website. Fatcow.com is no exception. In addition to providing basic website hosting for as little as $88 per year, this company also offers an inexpensive and easy-to-use e-commerce turnkey solution that allows credit card processing (for an additional fee) plus the tools necessary to build a basic, no-frills (but professional looking) e-commerce website quickly and inexpensively.

The ShopSite Manager toolkit, priced at $29.95 per month, allows you to develop an online store with an unlimited number of products. The ShopSite Pro service ($49.95 per month) offers additional features to make it easier to showcase products within your store, customize the site templates, and market your products. For someone planning to sell fewer than 15 products, the ShopSite Starter plan (included with basic website hosting services) is an ideal starting option.

All e-commerce sites created using ShopSite offer PayPal and Google Checkout compatibility (see Chapter 7). For an additional fee, you can obtain your own credit card merchant account and process real-time credit card transactions. To obtain a merchant account through FatCow.com (which ensures compatibility with your site), there is an additional fee of $19.95 per month, a fee of 2.19 percent of each total sale, and $.25 per transaction fee. A $25 monthly processing minimum also applies.

As you'd expect from a complete e-commerce turnkey solution, ShopSite requires absolutely no programming knowledge. A basic e-commerce website can be created and launched in just hours—not days or weeks. All of the tools needed to design, launch, and manage your site are online, so there's no need to purchase and install any specialized software for your computer.

To see a sampling of demo stores created using ShopSite, visit shopsite .com/demo.html. Fatcow, a website hosting and e-commerce turnkey solution provider, has been in business since 1998. According to the company's website, "We took a look around and saw lots of techno babble, confusing pricing schemes, and not much in the way of customer satisfaction or support. We decided that a simpler, more customer-friendly approach was needed . . . We've grown our company with a dedicated group of talented believers in the notion that simple, old-fashioned service and value still ring true."

GoDaddy.com's WebSite Tonight and Quick Shopping Cart

Service provider: GoDaddy

Website: godaddy.com

Turnkey solution pricing: $9.95 to $49.99 per month (plus additional fees)

In addition to being a well-established website hosting service and ISP, GoDaddy.com is also an inexpensive domain name registrar and offers a wide range of à la carte online tools for promoting and managing any type of website. For people interested in launching an online business that uses an e-commerce site (complete with shopping cart module), Go Daddy's turnkey solution is Quick Shopping Cart.

By default, the Quick Shopping Cart application can be fully customized and is compatible with PayPal and some independent credit card merchant accounts. For an additional fee, an online business operator can, however, obtain a merchant account through Go Daddy, which allows for secure, real-time credit card transactions.

The Economy Quick Shopping Cart application ($9.99 per month), which can be used to create a standalone e-commerce site or incorporated seamlessly into any website, allows a product catalog of up to 20 items. The plan includes 50 megabytes of online storage, plus one gigabyte of monthly bandwidth. The Deluxe Quick Shopping Cart ($29.00 per month) allows a product catalog with up to 100 items, including one gigabyte of online storage plus 50 gigabytes of bandwidth per month. In addition, the application can be integrated with QuickBooks.

For an online businessperson with a large selection of items and plans to expand her offerings over time, Go Daddy's Premium Edition Quick Shopping Cart ($49.99 per month) allows an unlimited products catalog, includes two gigabytes of online storage and 100 gigabytes per month of bandwidth, and has QuickBooks integration.

Go Daddy's Quick Shopping Cart allows secure online transactions and offers a variety of tools to customize the shoppers' experiences when they visit your site. The comprehensive selection of tools also allows you to properly manage your online business, track orders, and market your business. Using this service, you design the look of your store, add products to your catalog, and select shipping, payment, and tax options.

GoDaddy.com offers a menu of fee-based services for the e-commerce business operator, including basic website hosting and domain name registration. For low additional fees (charged monthly or annually), a shopping cart/e-commerce module (called Quick Shopping Cart) can be added to any website. You can also obtain a credit card merchant account through GoDaddy.com, and use the company's Traffic Blazer Plus service to kick off your search engine listing and optimization efforts and begin promoting your business.

GoDaddy.com has also bundled its online tools into a package designed specifically for e-commerce entrepreneurs. You can then add to this bundle by paying for additional services separately. For example, website hosting, combined with GoDaddy.com's Website Tonight website development tools, and the Economy Quick Shopping Cart are available as a bundle for an annual fee starting at just $155.54 per year.

There are several different options for establishing your own credit card merchant account through Go Daddy. A Standard Merchant Account allows you to accept orders from the United States only. There's a one-time application fee of $59.95, a monthly fee of $20, a discount rate of 2.59 percent per transaction, and a per-transaction fee of $.35.

Depending on what you're selling and if you want to accept orders from the United States and Canada, you may need to apply for a Specialty Merchant Account. The application fee is $199. There's also a $20 monthly fee, a discount rate of 2.39 percent per transaction, and a per-transaction fee of $.30.

An International Merchant Account allows you to accept and process credit card orders from virtually anywhere in the world. There's a $695 application fee, a $20 per month fee, a discount rate that starts at 4.95 percent per transaction, and a $.40 per-transaction fee.

Merchants receive the funds from credit card orders within 24 to 72 hours, and applications for merchant accounts are typically approved within one day. The merchant account you acquire through Go Daddy works seamlessly with the WebSite Tonight and Quick Shopping Cart applications and allows for secure online payment transactions.

Another nice feature of the Quick Shopping Cart application is that merchants can quickly sell items through eBay auctions (using a special Certified eBay listing tool). Go Daddy offers telephone and online technical support 24 hours per day, 7 days per week. Overall, this is one of the more robust and flexible e-commerce turnkey solutions available. And the services are offered at very competitive prices and are easy to use, with no programming required.

1&1 eShops

Service provider: 1&1 Internet Inc.

Phone number: (877) GO-1AND1

Website: order.1and1.com/xml/order/Eshops

Turnkey solution pricing: $5 to $25 per month (plus additional fees)

After recently celebrating its 20th anniversary in business (an extremely impressive achievement for any internet company), 1&1 Internet Inc. now boasts that it is the world's largest website hosting service. As such, it offers a variety of site hosting and development tools, as well as its powerful yet extremely inexpensive eShops service—a turnkey solution for developing an e-commerce site quickly and inexpensively.

Using the eShops online development tools, merchants can quickly and easily customize site templates to give their online store a unique but professional look and design. For someone with a bit more experience, a completely original design, without using a template, can also be created.

Starting at just $5 per month for a basic eShop capable of selling up to 50 different products, this is an excellent deal for someone getting started with an online business venture. Without possessing a merchant account, online payments through PayPal can automatically be used by your eShop site. You can also incorporate real-time credit card processing if you have your own merchant account.

According to the company, "1&1 provides a complete online store with no installation necessary. Build your eCommerce website with ease using our eShops. You can choose from more than 30 customizable, ready-to-go templates. We include a choice of payment/shipping methods, customer/invoice numbers and e-mail order confirmation. You also have the ability to check and administer your 1&1 eShop from anywhere and at any time. . . . You don't have to install anything because the shop software will automatically be set up for you. Depending on the particular package, each shop has a certain amount of disk space. Although a small part of this already has been used for the shop software, most of it is available for your data. There will be regular backups of your shop. . . . Your eShop can be set up step-by-step. There are several set-up wizards presented as pop-up windows, for basic settings, payment methods, shipping methods, etc. You can decide how the shipping costs should be calculated for each shipping method by setting a minimum shipping charge of your choice, and set different rates based on the total order amount. . . . Like the Control Panel, the eShop Administration pages are SSL encrypted. So confidential information, such as order book and customer administration, cannot be accessed by third parties."

1&1 Internet Inc. offers telephone and online technical support, 7 days per week, 24 hours per day. All of the online site design and management tools are easy to use, powerful, and allow people to establish their online businesses quickly and inexpensively. For someone using specialized software, such as Microsoft FrontPage to create her site, eShop is fully compatible with FrontPage extensions as well as other third-party software packages, such as Adobe DreamWeaver.

OSCommerce

Service provider: OSCommerce

Website: oscommerce.com

Turnkey solution pricing: Free (Site hosting not included)

If you're looking for extremely powerful and versatile e-commerce website development tools that allows you to create the most professional and highly functional online business possible, look no further than OSCommerce. Unlike the "turnkey solutions" described in this chapter, OSCommerce is downloadable software that runs on your computer. It can be used to design, publish, and maintain an e-commerce website.

Although OSCommerce is not a complete turnkey solution in that it does not offer online hosting services for your online business, it does provide a free collection of development tools. This is extremely powerful software, but it requires a learning curve and some basic programming knowledge to utilize it fully. An alternative is to take advantage of the free OSCommerce website templates available for e-commerce and simply customize them.

The good news is that because OSCommerce is so popular, you'll have no trouble finding extremely talented programmers with the know-how to fully customize your e-commerce site using this software. All of the documentation you need to get started is provided, free of charge, from the OSCommerce website.

According to the software's creators, "OSCommerce is an online shop e-commerce solution that offers a wide range of out-of-the-box features that allow online stores to be set up fairly quickly with ease, and is available for free as an Open Source-based solution released under the GNU General Public License.

"OSCommerce was started in March 2000 and has since matured to a solution that is currently powering more than 13,000 registered live shops

CLICK TIP

When hiring a freelance website designer or programmer, try to negotiate a flat-rate fee for a project, as opposed to an hourly fee. Flat-rate charges will typically save you money and help ensure your project gets completed in a timely manner.

around the world. The success of OSCommerce is secured by a great and active community where members help one another out and participate in development issues reflecting upon the current state of the project. You are more than welcome to contribute to the success of OSCommerce by helping out in the realization of the project, by participating in the forums, by donating to the team developers and sponsoring the project, or just by spreading the word!"

For a listing of online stores currently operating OSCommerce, visit shops.oscommerce.com. The OSCommerce software is much more powerful and customizable than many of the turnkey solutions described in this chapter, but it's also more difficult to use, especially if you're not techno-savvy.

OSCommerce templates are available from a wide range of sources. Some of these templates, which can be customized to meet your unique needs, are offered free of charge, while others are sold by their independent creators. To find OSCommerce templates online, using any internet search engine, enter the search phrase "OSCommerce templates" or visit one of these ten sites:

1. algozone.com
2. myoscommercetemplates.com
3. oscmax.com
4. oscommercecafe.com
5. oscommercetemplates.com
6. templatemonster.com/oscommerce-templates.php
7. templateworld.com/oscommerce.html
8. theoscommercestore.com
9. tornado-templates.com/oscommerce-templates.php
10. websitetemplatedesign.com

To have an e-commerce website created from scratch using the OSCommerce software or to have a template fully customized to meet the unique needs of your online business venture, you can find qualified programmers by using sites such as: eLance.com, getafreelancer.com, or Guru.com. Fees vary greatly, so be sure to shop around and carefully evaluate a website designer's portfolio before hiring him.

Yahoo! Stores (Yahoo! Small Business Solutions)

> Service provider: Yahoo!
>
> Phone number: (866) 781-9246
>
> Website: smallbusiness.yahoo.com/ecommerce
>
> Turnkey solution pricing: $39.95 to $299.95 per month (plus additional fees)

If you know anything about the internet or consider yourself an accomplished web surfer, you already know that Yahoo! is one of the most popular internet search engines and web directories. As a company, Yahoo! also offers a wide range of other services to internet users.

For online business operators, Yahoo! offers its Small Business Services division. It includes a robust e-commerce turnkey solution, called Yahoo! Stores as well as search engine marketing/advertising opportunities for promoting your online business (see Day 5: Marketing).

No matter which of the Yahoo! Stores plans you purchase, you'll be given full access to the service's Store Design tools, which allow you to design a professional-looking site using a step-by-step wizard and templates that can be fully customized. Using this solution, you can sell up to 50,000 unique products and maintain your online business with the utmost ease.

Included with each Yahoo! Stores package is a fully secure shopping cart and checkout application that can also be fully customized. Although you can incorporate your own merchant account to accept credit card payments, Yahoo! Merchant Solutions has a partnership with Chase Paymentech and PayPal to offer fully compatible merchant account and online credit card processing options (for an additional fee).

The turnkey solution offered by Yahoo! also features a vast array of tools for marketing your business and driving traffic to your website, and a variety of order processing, inventory management, website traffic reporting, and book-keeping tools to make fulfilling orders and managing your customers easier and less time consuming.

Through Yahoo! Stores, Yahoo! Merchant Solutions truly offers a comprehensive e-commerce turnkey solution that's affordable, expandable, easy to use, and highly functional when it comes to designing, launching, and operating your online business venture. Best of all, you can get your online store up and running in hours using the service's Store Design tools.

As you grow and expand your website beyond the capabilities of the design tools offered, you'll discover that Yahoo! Stores is fully compatible with popular third-party applications, such as Adobe Dreamweaver, Adobe GoLive, and Microsoft Office FrontPage. Telephone and online technical support is available 24 hours per day, 7 days per week.

Yahoo! Stores has three different price plans, including the $39.95 per month Starter Plan. For additional functionality, the Standard Plan ($99.95 per month) is offered. It is ideal for online businesses generating between $12,000 and $80,000 per month. The Professional Plan, which is ideal for businesses generating more than $80,000 per month, is available for $299.95 per month. Depending on the plan you purchase and whether you prepay for service, discounts to the monthly fees are available.

In addition to the monthly fee, Yahoo! Merchant Solutions charges a per-transaction fee of between .75 percent and 1.5 percent of each transaction, depending on the Yahoo! Stores plan you sign up for. This added per-transaction fee is in addition to any credit card processing fees you may be responsible for.

According to Yahoo!, the transaction fee is "a fee to maintain the infrastructure that supports your e-commerce services and transaction processing. This fee is based on the final price of the product and is not calculated on shipping and taxes. For comparison, some large e-commerce companies spend roughly five to eight percent of their sales to maintain their e-commerce infrastructure. We charge just .75 to 1.5 percent for access to similar e-commerce infrastructure and services of a similar level of quality."

Because Yahoo! Merchant Solutions is so popular, you'll find many independent freelance programmers who can help you customize and design your website, incorporating functionality and features that go beyond what's offered using the supplied Store Design tools. For a listing of pre-approved programming professionals (additional fees will apply for their services), visit developernetwork.store.yahoo.com.

Currently thousands of online-based businesses operate using Yahoo! Stores. To see a sampling of these stores and what yours could look like, visit smallbusiness.yahoo.com/ecommerce/customerstores.php.

The tools and services offered by Yahoo! Small Business Services are among the most powerful and cost-effective in the industry. You'll find that Yahoo! Merchant Services is equipped to handle the needs of almost every type of online business venture, yet the tools are easy-to-use, even for non-techno-savvy people.

When You Are Ready to Grow Beyond Your Turnkey Solution

If you opt to use a complete e-commerce turnkey solution and your online-based business becomes successful, at some point your needs as well as the demands of your customers may grow beyond the capability of the online tools provided by your turnkey solution. When this happens, give yourself a pat on the back. You've officially become a successful and accomplished e-commerce entrepreneur who is operating a profitable online business venture.

To be able to grow and expand your website, it may become necessary to use third-party website creation and management tools, such as Adobe Dreamweaver. Using these programs, however, requires some basic programming knowledge, and there's a learning curve for proficiency with the applications. To make the transition seamless, you'll probably want to hire freelance programmers and/or website designers who can handle much of the technical stuff for you. To learn more about some of the popular third-party website development tools available, visit these websites:

➡ Adobe Creative Suite 4—adobe.com/products/creativesuite
➡ Adobe Dreamweaver CS4—adobe.com/products/dreamweaver

➡ Adobe Flash—adobe.com/products/flash

➡ Adobe Photoshop CS4—adobe.com/products/photoshop/family

➡ eCommerce—oscommerce.com

➡ LaGarde—storefront.net

➡ Lite Commerce—litecommerce.com

➡ Merchandizer—merchandizer.com

➡ Microsoft Office FrontPage—office.microsoft.com/en-us/frontpage/default.aspx

➡ Microsoft SharePoint Designer 2007—office.microsoft.com/en-us/sharepointdesigner

What's Next?

Once you've selected a turnkey solution that you believe is best suited to the needs of your gift business venture, you need to begin designing the look of your website and creating its content. In Day 4: Website Design you are introduced to the important design fundamentals for creating a website that looks professional, is easy to navigate, is welcoming to your customers, turns visits into orders, and provides the functionality needed for your business to become successful.

Chapter 5

Day 4: Website Design

*Y*ou have dealt with a lot of the website design issues in your early thinking and as you looked at choosing a turnkey solution to having an online gift store. However, in this chapter we cover general website design issues as well as specific issues:

➡ How do you shoot and acquire product photos?

➡ How do you introduce new products?

➡ How do you acquire links?

Many website design issues overlap with general marketing issues, which are covered in Day 5.

CLICK TIP

Just because you've chosen to use a turnkey solution for a website does not mean it has to be a cookie cutter site. There are lots of ways to customize even a template—color, typeface, and simply the products you have for sale help create a custom design.

Appealing to Your Buyer

When potential buyers walk into a Cadillac showroom, they expect to have an experience of a different caliber compared to what they would encounter if they were shopping at their local Ford dealership. Harley Davidson motorcycle dealerships are spotless works of art; they know that their middle-aged customer base is almost completely different from, say, the young dirt bike buyer. Check out websites of different products you are familiar with and get a sense of how these sites cater to their buyer base. Think about the customers you want to attract as you build your website in both design and product offering.

Website Design

You have three main goals when designing a website intended for commerce:

1. It must be visually attractive to the user.
2. It must be extremely easy to navigate.
3. It must be as informative as you can possibly make it.

In other words, every detail of your website must work together smoothly and efficiently to provide your customers with a clear view of your marketing message, be in keeping with your company's image and credibility, and make it easy for customers to place their orders.

CLICK TIP

Web browsers have a short attention span. They expect things to happen fast—the internet has trimmed patience down to a few seconds. Don't load your website up with complicated features and high-quality photos that slow down the process of moving through the site. You will lose lots of customers that way.

The design of your site should be simple yet comprehensive. By the time your customers have spent a few minutes on your website, they should have a pretty good sense of your business—not just what you sell but that you care about quality and customer service.

Your Homepage

Your customers first come to your homepage, where you introduce them to your business and tempt them to spend some time on your site browsing other pages—and ultimately be enticed enough to order something. This is where your logo, if you have one, begins to be imprinted on your customers' brains. Even the simplest things such as what typeface your name is in or what colors you use begin the branding process. If you use hot pink Comic Sans type, everyone who visits your website more than once is going to associate hot pink Comic Sans typeface with your business.

On your homepage, you should give a little history about how you got started but don't tell every detail about every thought you've ever had about the business. This is a chance for customers to feel they know you, but you don't want to get them to that "too much information" stage! Remember, you can lose them as quickly as it takes you to say the word "click."

You'll want photos of a couple of your key products on your homepage. Don't go for the sale items—announce any sale you are having on your homepage but the items you put on sale are probably there because they are not your biggest sellers. That's not the image you want potential customers to have when they get to your site.

Web customers should open to your site and know they got the site they are looking for. Go ahead and include a shot of you and your dog who accompanies you to work every day, but don't forget to show the gift items you want to be known for!

You don't need and don't want to show every item you sell right when the customer arrives at your site. With too many photos and high-quality graphics, your homepage can take too long to load onto your potential customer's computer; she might move on to another website before even seeing any of your products. Keep the homepage simple but informative and enticing.

By all means, do some advertising on this page. "Did you know that May 6th is National Nurses Day" or some other blurb that makes the viewer really think about ordering a specific gift is a great way to push from simply viewing of your site to an actual order.

Include a menu of items along one edge of your homepage with headings that the customer can click on to get to that section of your online store. Think of your menu as the signs you see overhead in a grocery store or the pharmacy—directing customers to the sections they are interested in. Use words with which they are familiar and use these "signs" as an opportunity to remind them of what you have and what they might need.

Drilling Down

Each time viewers click on a button on your website, they get further into your site. Movement into your site can be accomplished in two ways—one is with a "pop-up window." When visitors click on a category, the new section pops up over the main page, and then when they are done browsing it and close it out, they are brought back to the page they started from. The other technique "drills" them further and further into your site, so they have to backtrack through the pages to get back to where they were. Drilling down is a common way for websites to be set up, but it can get frustrating to your customers if they can't easily get back to a point where they saw something they wanted to look at further. One way to help here is to always have a "home" button on every page—all people have to do is click "home" to get them back to the beginning. They can find their way forward again from there. It's like having Dorothy's ruby red slippers at their fingertips at all times.

WARNING

Do not include a hit counter on your site. You want to know this information but you don't want to advertise it to your competitors. Customers might question your credibility or popularity if your hit counter increases by only a few customers from one time they visit to the next.

Each of your gifts should have its own page. If you sell lines of gifts—several items from one jewelry designer, for example—you should plan to have a button for customers to click on that takes them to that line. The page that comes up could showcase all the products from that line; then by clicking on each product, they get detailed information about that one item. A similar system could be helpful for pottery, woodcrafts, or items that have a theme, such as dogs or motorcycles.

Specifics

What do customers want to see when they click on a gift item on your site? They want to see as much detail as possible. The main thing that still turns customers away from ordering online is the lack of the touchy-feely experience. When people are ordering something that is the same no matter what— dog food, cosmetic products, printer ink—they don't need to pick it up and feel it, turn it over in their hands, and inspect the bottom. But when you are asking customers to take your word that a gift item is a quality product, you need to back up your word with as much information as possible.

In addition, you should keep in mind that the buyer is probably giving this purchase as a gift to someone else—perhaps sight unseen by them ever! They are putting a lot of faith in your judgment. Once they have a great experience, of course, that is no longer a problem.

You can help customers through this negative aspect of online purchasing by showing multiple views of your gift items. If the item is something that is worn, show someone wearing it. If it comes in several colors, allow the viewer to click on different colors and see the item in the various possibilities. Pottery

> ## CLICK TIP
>
> ALWAYS include the ability to purchase gift certificates on your website. Make this button clear and simple. Most times people would rather buy an actual gift for the recipient to unwrap, but the gift certificate is the escape route for those who are buying a gift for someone in a topic of interest that is outside their own realm of knowledge.

items could have a bottom view to show marks and signatures. Photograph decorative items such as wall hangings or lamps being used decoratively.

To depict something as extremely soft, show it with a baby. To show that it is waterproof, like a watch, photograph someone wearing the watch while canoeing or watering the garden. Be creative and really get a potential customer's attention by showing proof of your claims.

Another problem you need to overcome is that a lot of gift buyers are buying gifts in categories they know nothing about. For example, a mother might be buying her son the motorcyclist a gift from your motorcycling site. Any information like "Great for that motorcyclist who is on the road rain or shine" can help your customer figure out if this is an appropriate purchase for the person she or he has in mind. Anything you can do to help viewers make decisions and envision the gift in the hands of the person they are planning to gift it to helps make your sale.

The Rest of the Site

Your homepage is one of the most important parts of your website. From there, depending on what kind of gift site you are creating, you might want to show different kinds of gifts under different buttons on the homepage. So when a customer clicks on the "Holiday Gifts" button, they see samples of gifts you offer that are appropriate for Mother's Day, Christmas, Hanukkah, Easter, or whatever. Other buttons might be "Men's Gifts," "Corporate Gifts," or "Food Gifts."

Some added-value pages you could include are a calendar showing all the national "celebration days" such as Nurses' Day, Doctors' Day, and

Grandparents' Day to remind visitors of days they might want to plan to buy a gift for. A page of "testimonials" from your regular customers is always a good marketing tool. Again, depending on the type of gift business you are setting up, you might have a few buttons that lead people to gifts by price such as "$25," or "$50 to $100."

Key Pages to Include

For your online gift business, you need to be sure that visitors to your website are provided with all the information they need to make a purchase. The following are the most common individual web pages that should be incorporated into your site and the type of content that should be incorporated within each.

- ➡ *Blog, podcast, or newsletter.* One way to enhance customer loyalty, teach people more about your products, increase repeat orders, and build brand awareness is to offer a regularly published (daily, weekly, or monthly) blog, podcast, or downloadable newsletter that not only communicates your marketing message but also includes information that is valuable to your customers: how-to articles or tips for saving time or money when using your product. While you can offer these as a free download from your website, you can also have an opt-in e-mail list that people subscribe to in order to have your blog, podcast, or newsletter sent directly to their inbox, which gets you a little more targeted attention.

- ➡ *Company Information, About Us, or Company Background.* Tell your company's story, describe its philosophies, explain why your company and its products are different from your competition, and illustrate how your products are unique or special. You can also include short biographies of your company's executives, which helps to build credibility. Don't go overboard with this—this is where a little goes a long way. Keep your company information down to one screen.

- ➡ *Contact Us.* One of the most powerful ways you can quickly build potential customers' confidence in your business and gain credibility is to make your company completely transparent. Make yourself available to answer questions, address concerns, and handle problems. In addition to displaying a toll-free telephone number, be sure to display your company's full mailing address and e-mail address. If you have a customer service department, returns department, public relations/marketing department, or advertising department, list contact information for each division separately. Making your customers feel that they can reach you easily if they experience problems or have questions gives them more confidence in placing an order.

➡ *Customer testimonials*. Offering a page that reproduces customer testimonials relating to your company and its products is a great way to increase a potential customer's confidence and enhance your company's credibility. Keep the testimonials short and to the point, but make sure they're positive, believable, accurate, truthful, and informative.

➡ *FAQ*. Frequently Asked Question pages usually adhere to a question-and-answer format and are used to answer the most common questions potential customers have. They save you and your customers time by making it easy for them to get these common questions answered without having to make a separate call and talk with someone. No matter how straightforward and easy to understand the information about your products and your company's policies are, visitors to your website will still have questions about pricing, product specifications, how to place an order, and return policies. Once you have created this text, be sure to have a few people who are not so familiar with your company read it and confirm that it is clear and easily understood. You can create separate FAQ documents that describe: how to use your product, the top features of a specific product, how to place an order, your company's return policies, or answers to the most common questions your customers have.

➡ *News, sales, and promotions*. This page of your website can be used just like a weekly circular or print advertisement to promote news about your company and its products, and sales or promotions.

➡ *Online ordering/shopping cart*. When visitors are ready to place an order for your products, they click on a Buy Now or Order icon, for example, and get linked to your site's shopping cart. The shopping cart is an online order form that allows your customers to input their order-related information (including their payment details) and have the order processed (often in real time). The turnkey website solution you use will include a shopping cart, but it's essential that the shopping cart application built into your site be easy to use and include all of the functionality that's necessary for your customers to quickly place their orders online.

➡ *Press room.* Part of your business's success strategy should be to use a public relations campaign to generate publicity about your business and its products (see Chapter 6). The Press Room area of your website should contain an online press kit, copies of press releases, high-resolution product photography, and contact information for members of the media (reporters, journalists, and editors) to reach you quickly. When members of the media are working on stories, they're typically under very tight deadlines. If you make all the information they need available on your site, your chances of receiving free publicity and having your products mentioned in articles, features, or news stories increase dramatically. The Press Room area can also be used to showcase publicity your company or its products have already received.

➡ *Product description/catalog pages.* Your gift product description and/or catalog pages are absolutely critical. It's here your customers learn about the products you're offering through detailed, well-written descriptions and by viewing product photography. Although you want to keep your product descriptions relatively short, they must also be comprehensive, informative, accurate, and easy to understand, and contain all the details customers will want to know before they place their order. All of your product descriptions should be consistent in format and tone, and should be aimed specifically to the primary audience you have chosen to target. You want to include a Buy, Order, or Add to Cart icon with each product description so people can quickly order the product online. Don't make it difficult for customers to order! It should be as simple as saying "That's nice and would be perfect for Aunt Loreen for Christmas." You might also opt to include customer reviews of your products.

➡ *Return Policy/Guarantee/Warrantee.* Displaying product-specific information for your customers is another way to boost their confidence before they place their order. An important aspect of good customer service is explaining upfront how your company handles problems and a customer's need or desire to return products. If you charge a restocking fee for returns or issue refunds within 15 days, these policies should be spelled out on your site. Keep in mind that your customers will appreciate a 30-day, no-questions-asked, unconditional return policy with no restocking fee. The easier it is for customers to handle returns, the more confident they'll be in taking a chance on buying products, sight unseen, from your website.

→ *Splash page.* Avoid these fancy opening animation pages that are supposed to make a splash and cause visitors to go "wow"! Some sites use them to introduce people to their website. The problem with splash pages is that they look great, but take valuable time to load and typically say absolutely nothing about the company or its products. In other words, for most online gift websites, they're an utter waste of time. Today's customer has seen it all—the "wow factor" has to be very high to make a regular internet user go "wow." And if potential customers have to wait even five seconds for a site's splash page to load, you run a great risk of losing them before they've even visited your site. Remember, they are visiting your site to learn about and/or buy a product, not to be entertained.

→ *Technical Support/Customer Service.* Depending on what you're selling, it may be necessary or appropriate to offer ongoing technical support to existing customers via telephone and online through live chats or e-mail, for example. Having an area of your website dedicated to helping customers use your products once they order them improves customer loyalty and helps generate repeat orders. It also increases your chances of receiving positive word-of-mouth advertising. One of your ongoing goals in terms of your business operations should be to provide the most professional, helpful, friendly, and accessible customer service possible. In some cases, customers go out of their way or pay more for products if they know they'll be supported by top-notch customer service or technical support from the company they make the purchase from. You can get this support information from the companies whose products you carry.

CLICK TIP

Always include your business's name, address, and phone number on every page of your website. Once customers have drilled a few pages down into your site, they don't want to have to backtrack all the way back to your homepage just to get your contact information.

Selling from a Website

It used to be that businesses used websites mainly as marketing pieces—people came to the site to view your products, then either called an order in or printed out a order form from the site and faxed their order to you. Those days are almost gone. Customers expect to be able to sit at their computer and not only see what you have to offer but also to be able to order it right then and there. If they can't, there is a good chance you are going to lose them to another site where they can.

Online ordering is covered in detail in Chapter 7, but right now you need to know that the two key attributes your site needs—and that your designer or your template will set you up with—are a shopping cart for customers to collect their items in and a secure way to pay for them.

Shopping Cart

The shopping cart is a simple function that your web designer builds into your site if you say you want it (which you do). As your online customers shop, they can click the little button that says "add this item to my shopping cart," and it will join the other items they have already put in the cart. Some carts accumulate items that stay there even after the customers have left the site. This feature can translate into more sales—if customers get interrupted before completing the transaction, they don't have to go through the entire shopping process when they return to your site. "Abandoned" shopping carts are a big issue with online shopping. Saving carts can retrieve some of those abandoned carts.

The shopping cart page is where customers can make changes. Here they can change the quantity of each item (sometimes bad for you, when they decide to change it to zero, other times good when they decide not only will they order one of these bracelets for their sister, but they will change the quantity to three and send one to Mom and Aunt Jean as well).

The shopping cart page is also where customers decide what kind of shipping they want. Always offer inexpensive shipping options along with overnight options—shipping costs still bog down catalog and online sales. Give customers the option of making it very cheap. But you also want them to feel they can shop online at the last minute as well, so the ability to have something shipped overnight is a must.

Payment

Once your customer has filled her shopping cart, she is going to need to pay for her purchases. Chapter 7 covers this in detail, but as you build your website you need to be sure to provide customers not only with several payment options—various credit cards, PayPal, etc.—but you also need to be sure it is perfectly clear to your customers that their purchase is totally secure. Simply stating "check out now on our secure service" is one way to do that. Another is to include your security choice's symbol—like VeriSign—on your site. Make sure your entire website is professional looking, neat, and organized to give customers further confidence in your site.

Product Display

The more you can show about your gifts, the more likely your site's visitors will click on the "order" button. The hardest part about online ordering, as we've discussed, is that "sight unseen, no-touchy-feely" aspect. You need to do everything you can to offset that.

Bling

When photographing products, figure out what features are the most important to potential customers and make sure you show those features. If a diamond needs to sparkle, photograph it to catch the light and sparkle. If it is important that the color of the item is the blackest of black, photograph it on a white background and make it say black loud and clear. If it is a product that moves, move it and photograph it moving! If softness is the key, make sure you use props that show how soft this fabric really is.

Clarity

It should go without saying, but if you can't take clear pictures, find someone who can. Imagine the enthusiasm of a visitor to your site if they are trying to decide on a gift for a loved one by looking at fuzzy pictures of the items available.

You might also be able to get your product shots from the manufacturer. The last thing you want to do is to spoil a purchase because the product photo was low quality and unimpressive to the viewer. It doesn't take as much for a screen-viewed photo to look pretty nice compared to a print photo. Shoot your photos in at least 300 dpi (dots-per-inch, known as "resolution"; the more dots-per-inch, the better the resolution, the sharper the photo) and make sure they are in focus.

Backdrop

Don't clutter your photos with complicated backgrounds. Unless you are shooting jewelry or clothing being worn by models, use plain fabrics for a backdrop. Make sure the fabric is ironed. And use colors that showcase, not camouflage, the item.

Lighting

Lighting is critical. Have enough light to avoid casting shadows, unless you want to use shadows for special effect. Pay attention to windows and glass and the glare that they can cause. Depending on the size of your products, set up a small photo studio in the corner of your office or warehouse with just what you need to create great photographs. Purchase some task lights with large metal pans that flood the light on the overall product; they are inexpensive and make all the difference. Have a supply of different color fabrics and hang them on a rod so that you won't have to iron them every time you need to use one. Keep tape and pins nearby to hold things down if need be. Have a penny and a ruler that you can use to indicate an item's size.

Up Close

If an item has engraving, showcase the engraving. You might want to provide a detailed shot as well as an overview shot of anything that has fine detail that would lend itself to a potential purchase. For instance, perhaps a handmade wool sweater has unique buttons—show a shot of the sweater, preferably on a model, and provide the potential customer with the option of clicking on one of the buttons to pop up a window showing just the unique button. This is how you can show detail and close the sale without you and the customer being in the same room. But make it obvious that the buttons can be viewed by clicking on this or that icon. Don't hide these sales tools. These details define the unique gift items you have searched far and wide for and help make the sale.

Top Ten Website Design Tips

Here are ten tips you want to consider throughout the website design process. Designing your website is an art and a science. Just like with a brick-and-mortar store, where you would consider customer flow, color schemes, point-of-purchase items, and signage, so too you need to consider these kinds of things with your online gift site.

Tip 1: Design the Site to Be Visually Simple

The fonts, type styles, text colors, background colors, photographs, and other graphic elements you incorporate into your site contribute to its overall appearance. Your goal is to create a professional and appealing look for your turnkey solution site by customizing the template you're working with. Putting too much information on a page, using text that's too small or difficult to read, or using a color scheme that's not visually appealing or has too many colors detract from the experience your visitors have and the ease with which they can use your site. If you look at some of the most successful e-commerce sites such as Amazon.com, Target.com, or Apple.com, you'll notice that despite the fact that they sell a bajillion products, their layout is extremely simple, inviting, and visually appealing. While you never want to copy another site exactly, you can take design ideas from other sites and incorporate them into your own with proper customization.

Tip 2: Make Your Site Easy to Navigate

Confuse them and you'll lose them, it's as simple as that. Visitors are always one click away from surfing another site, probably your competitor's. No matter where on your site visitors happen to be, it should be obvious to them where they should go next or how they can quickly return to where they just were. If they're looking for something specific on your site, such as your product's features or your company's return policy, they should be able to find that information intuitively and quickly.

Tip 3: Avoid Pointless Effects

Just because you can add animations, video footage, sound effects, and other eye-catching effects to your site, it doesn't mean you should. They are often unnecessary and not beneficial. Focus on the very best way to communicate your particular sales message and educate people about your products using the simplest and quickest methods possible. If you can't write about a product without using at least three paragraphs, this is the time to hire a freelance copywriter to do that for you. Special effects most often simply distract visitors, waste their time while they're waiting for a useless animation to load, or confuse them. If your website is entertainment-oriented or your gift product is computer games, animation might be a necessity. But typically, when people are trying to learn about a product or make a purchase, they want the process to happen efficiently.

Tip 4: Use Professional-Quality Product Photos and Artwork

It can't be said enough: visitors to your site can't touch and feel your products as they could in a traditional retail store, so they rely on your product photographs to learn about the product. The photographs you use must be crystal clear, enlargeable (with a click of the mouse), detailed, and accompanied by an accurate depiction of what you're selling. For this reason, seriously consider using custom photographs created by a professional photographer or pictures from the manufacturer of your products (if you can obtain permission to use this artwork).

You probably want to learn how to take quality photographs, but as you're attempting to launch your online business, you may decide you have more important uses for your time. For a few hundred dollars, you can hire a professional photographer to provide you with the quality product photos you need.

To complement your custom product photography, you can use images on your website that you license and acquire from a stock photo agency. Agencies can supply professional images depicting almost anything. And your product suppliers are often able to supply you with product shots—the downside here is that in your efforts to create just the atmosphere you want to create with your website design, you are at the mercy of the product manufacturer or stock photo company's look.

Tip 5: Provide Contact Information

A great thing about cyberspace is that you can operate your online gift site from anywhere and potentially attract shoppers from all over the world. For some people, buying a product sight unseen from a company they can't physically visit is extremely intimidating. And, many people are concerned about credit card fraud and identity theft that might result from shopping with credit cards online.

In addition to creating a professional-looking and informative site that boosts confidence, one of the easiest ways to eliminate many of the fears people have about online shopping is to offer them an opportunity to make direct contact with you by telephone, e-mail, online chat, or U.S. mail. Again, don't be invisible. If someone can pick up the phone, dial a toll-free number, and quickly get questions answered or concerns addressed, he'll be more willing to shop from your site and become a customer.

CLICK TIP

When a customer—often still merely a *potential* customer—does contact you, you must provide topnotch customer service. Be professional, helpful, efficient, and friendly. And get them the answers to their concerns.

Tip 6: Be Honest

Everything on your site should be focused on communicating the absolute truth to your customers. If your product descriptions, product photographs, company background information, or any other content on your site doesn't come across as being upfront and honest, you'll lose credibility and your visitors will simply shop elsewhere. Sure, it's OK to use colorful language to advertise and market your product. However, never embellish the truth, make false statements, make promises you can't keep, or intentionally mislead your potential customers. Have outside readers review any product copy you create and have them ask tough questions about what your copy says and tell you how it comes across.

If someone receives the product they've ordered from your company and it doesn't live up to the expectations you helped create based on information on your website, it will be returned. When this happens, not only will you have lost a customer, but chances are, he'll tell other people about his negative experience dealing with you.

Tip 7: Communicate What Potential Customers Want to Know

The easiest way to convey information is to put yourself in your customers' shoes and think carefully about their wants and needs. This book has covered how to get to know your target customers. As you create the content for your website, focus on communicating your information quickly and efficiently, knowing the attention span of your visitors is short. This is another area where using outside readers and having people visit your site before it goes live helps you see the site outside your own unavoidably biased perspective.

Tip 8: Proofread

It's essential that you carefully and repeatedly proofread the content on your site. It should contain absolutely no typos or errors. Depending on the amount of text, this is another area where you might choose to hire a freelancer. Look for a professional editor to proofread the content of your site before it goes live. At the very least, have several people (in addition to yourself) proofread everything carefully.

Fix all typographical or grammatical errors in your text, and make sure all the photo captions describe the appropriate photos, the graphics are placed correctly, the photos are the right ones for the right captions, and the links on your page lead to the correct destinations. Web surfers find it extremely frustrating to click on a dead link or one that leads to the wrong place. Even the smallest errors on your site detract from the professional image you're trying to establish.

Tip 9: Make Your Site Compatible with the Common Web Browsers

There are only a handful of commonly used web browsers out there: Microsoft Explorer, Mozilla's FireFox, and Apple's Safari. And although Netscape Navigator is no longer formally supported, plenty of web surfers still use it as their primary browser.

Each of these browsers is slightly different, so it's important to take basic compatibility issues into consideration when designing your website or customizing a template. Before opening for business, test your site using each popular web browser, and be sure to fix any formatting or compatibility issues.

The AnyBrowser.com website (anybrowser.com) offers a collection of free tools and online resources designed for site publishers to help make sites compatible with all popular browsers. Keynote's Net Mechanic (netmechanic .com/ products/Browser-Tutorial.shtml) also offers tools for making a site compatible with all popular web browsers and offers tutorials for overcoming incompatibility issues between browsers.

Tip 10: Start Your Business with Enough Capital

Just because you are an online business, which by nature means you avoid a few of the common business money suckers like a storefront retail space, don't be fooled into thinking you don't need to pay close attention to your startup capital needs.

If you're a first-time online business owner, you can certainly start off small by offering one or just a few products initially, and focus on selling

CLICK TIP

Keep in mind that just because you are web savvy enough to be starting an online business, not all of your customers will be. And you may think that because you are selling the latest and greatest complex, in-demand computer games, your customer base is going to be intensely computer literate—but don't forget, if you are promoting your site as a gift site, those buyers who are purchasing gifts may not be the computer savvy folks!

those products to your target audience. As your business becomes successful, you can branch out by offering more products or product variations, and begin targeting a larger customer base.

Every business, including an online one, has a learning curve associated with getting it up and running. It also takes time for your business to be profitable. As you develop your business plan and preliminary budget, determine how much money it'll take to launch your business and keep it running for 6 to 12 months without generating a profit. How quickly your business becomes profitable depends on a wide range of factors, including the profit margin associated with the products you're selling.

In addition to establishing a realistic startup and operating budget, be sure to plan for the unexpected. There will be added costs and fees along the way that didn't get included in your first budget but will need to be covered to successfully launch and operate your business. Having enough money on hand to cover all the costs associated with running your business until it becomes profitable could mean the difference between ultimate success and failure. If you have to start cutting corners and taking short cuts to keep your business going or just to get it launched, your chances of encountering obstacles and problems increase exponentially.

Bonus Tip

OK, there's one more important tip you need: Know what your customer's surfing capabilities are. Believe it or not, not all web surfers access the internet using a high-speed DSL, Broadband, or FIOS connection. In fact, according to

Leichtman Research Group, in 2007, of the 53 percent of American homes that had access to the internet, around 47 percent (about 33 million U.S. users) still use a slow, dial-up connection. According to its report, "Broadband adoption is affected by household income. Broadband reaches 68 percent of households with annual income over $50,000. By contrast, 39 percent of households with income under $50,000 subscribe to broadband services."

Thanks to improving technologies, lower prices, and the growing popularity of the internet, Jupiter Research reports that adoption of high-speed internet services is expected to reach 70 percent of all U.S. households by 2012. So surfing capabilities are going to improve soon.

In the meantime, make sure your site (or a version of your site) works well for people using a slow internet connection. Also, avoid incorporating features into your site that require browser plug-ins that aren't common. Although many web surfers have added a Flash player and/or PDF file reader plug-in to their browser, there are plenty of plug-ins that are far less popular. If your site requires the use of a less popular plug-in, you will greatly reduce the number of web surfers capable of visiting and ordering from your site. Focus on catering to the broadest audience of web surfers possible, unless you know that the majority of people in your target audience are web savvy and utilize a high-speed connection.

Chapter 6

Day 5: Marketing

*A*nything that is sold needs to be marketed. Potential customers need to know that you have the product and they need to be told why they need to buy it. And why they need to buy it from you.

If you plan to sell thousands of gifts in your online store, you will not be able to put your digital marketing materials together in a day. But if you plan to start with 10 to 20 high-quality items, here's what you will learn in this chapter:

➡ How do you write marketing copy that sells?

➡ What extras do you need to provide to help online customers make a decision?

➡ How do you make potential customers aware of your gift store?

The Marketing Plan

You did a business plan and your business plan included a section on marketing. But if you want to have enough customers to succeed and eventually grow your business, you should develop a separate marketing plan. A marketing plan allows you to

➡ chart growth in the gift industry,

➡ define the market you serve,

➡ define your customers,

➡ determine the strengths and weaknesses of the competition,

➡ project sales,

➡ establish strategies to achieve your marketing goals, and

➡ establish a market niche.

That's a lot of important stuff!

Your marketing plan should consist of

➡ an executive summary about yourself and any key personnel,

➡ a description of your gift business/line,

➡ goals and objectives,

➡ a market analysis,

➡ a description of your customers,

➡ an analysis of your business' competition,

➡ marketing tactics,

➡ advertising plans,

➡ financial projections, and

➡ a summary of your business.

Plan to use a combination of straight narrative as well as a chart or two. Most of the latest office software includes the ability to automatically make a pie chart or graph out a spreadsheet. This isn't just for looks. It allows you a more dramatic way of looking at a collection of numbers. Seeing the figures showing your customers as 17 percent in their 20s, 20 percent in their 30s, and 63 percent over 40 is less impressive than seeing that big old chunk of the pie chart devoted to the over-40 customer.

Make Customer Service a Marketing Tool

There is probably no business where customer service works better as a marketing tool than in gift purchasing. But what does customer service mean in the online world? This is where the pages on your website make all the difference.

Your FAQ page is customer service. It provides potential customers with immediate answers to common questions so they don't have to spend extra time calling you for the information.

Being thorough with the amount of information you provide on each of your products is customer service. Describing fabric, size, and features assist customers in making a decision. Being able to see a sweater in several different colors with just a click of a mouse is like having the store clerk there to bring it to you from the rack.

Then, of course, there is the traditional customer service—when the customer picks up the phone and asks you to explain something, help with a purchase, or address a concern. Whoever answers those calls needs to know all the traditional customer service techniques to keep that person as a customer. They include

- being sympathetic to the customer's concern,
- being friendly and attentive, not grumpy and distracted,
- knowing the information or directing the customer to someone who does,
- familiarity with the products sold on your gift website,
- offering a solution,
- offering compensation for the customer's trouble—a discount certificate, free shipping of a replacement item, or whatever is most valuable to that customer, and
- encouraging the customer to come back with incentives like discounts and specials.

Marketing Your Website

Once you have created your gift website, don't keep it a secret! This is especially important if your online gift store is an adjunct business to a brick-and-mortar store.

These are just a few of a long list of ideas for getting people to come to your website in the first place, to keep coming back, and to encourage them to tell everyone they know. Click around to websites in the gift industry in any

GET PEOPLE CLICKING

There's no point to having a website if you don't do what you can to get people to click on it. Here are some tips for attracting visitors, and possibly buyers, to your website:

- Simply tell all your friends and family and ask them to tell all their friends and family.

- Do the appropriate search engine registration.

- Make sure every printed and online piece you send to anyone has your website URL listed prominently.

- Suggest visitors bookmark your site.

- Trade web advertising with other websites.

- Create contests with giveaways.

- Change your content/product regularly to keep people coming back to see what's new.

- Join online discussion groups.

- If you do public speaking, always mention your site.

- Provide an "expert" column to newspapers and make sure to mention your website.

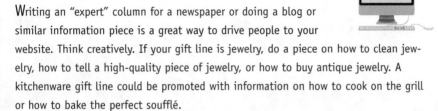

CLICK TIP

Writing an "expert" column for a newspaper or doing a blog or similar information piece is a great way to drive people to your website. Think creatively. If your gift line is jewelry, do a piece on how to clean jewelry, how to tell a high-quality piece of jewelry, or how to buy antique jewelry. A kitchenware gift line could be promoted with information on how to cook on the grill or how to bake the perfect soufflé.

category that interests you, see what catches your eye, and get other creative ideas to drive people to your site.

E-Newsletters

Creating a newsletter that is sent via e-mail has become a popular way for businesses to keep in touch with their customers. An e-mail newsletter is a little reminder to your customers that you are there and waiting to fulfill their gift needs.

Solicit e-newsletter subscribers on your own website and on the websites of others. Sending e-newsletters out unsolicited is considered "spam" and can land you in a bit of hot water. But once you create a useful, readable newsletter that might even contain a coupon, a special, or even a giveaway, people will readily subscribe.

Keep 'Em Interested

Once you get visitors checking out your site, there are some ways to keep them there as long as possible. The longer they are there, the more likely they are to order something.

Be sure they know immediately whose website they have gotten to. Make it easy for them to contact you by having a "contact us" button that makes it simple for them to send you a message.

Keep your website fun and changing. Do contests, include puzzles, whatever you can for fun interaction but always connect it to your gift business.

NETIQUETTE

The dramatic increase in the use of e-mail means there is a need to understand good etiquette when it comes to e-mailing. The last thing you want to do is offend a customer. So follow these guidelines for proper e-mailing:

- Never use all uppercase letters; it is considered the equivalent of shouting.

- Spell check your e-mails. Just because e-mail is quick, it doesn't have to be sloppy.

- Give an accurate sense of what your e-mail is about in the subject line.

- Create a signature for your e-mail so that every e-mail you compose automatically includes your business name, address, phone number, and e-mail address so the recipient can quickly see how to contact you.

- Keep your messages short and to the point.

Provide site visitors with added value such as information sheets that have some connection with your gift selection. (Don't forget to get permission and credit any information you use from elsewhere.)

Make it easy for customers on your website to order and pay. Nothing makes visitors click the exit button faster than to find it is difficult to spend their money!

Paid Advertising

The other side of the marketing coin is paid advertising. Free publicity garnered through your efforts at writing articles and sending press releases is the

CLICK TIP

Consider customizing your gift products. Anything from dog beds to hair clips to scarves can be customized. This makes your gift products stand out as even more special. Be sure to price accordingly!

best there is—first, it is free, and second, editorial content is considered by readers to have more clout because it is not in your biased words, but the word of the medium covering the topic.

Paid advertising is under your control—you decide what it says, how it looks, how long it is, what it sounds like, even when it is seen or heard. It is valuable and worth carefully crafting an advertising campaign—free publicity is fantastic, but you can't count on it. You can count on paid advertising.

Advertising can be expensive. In order for it to be effective, you need to do it with some frequency and regularity. Customers must view your ad multiple times before they actually click on your website. Be sure your marketing plan includes your advertising plans.

It is a bit of a science to know where to put your advertising dollars. You need to be where your potential customers—your "target audience"—are going

ADVERTISING LINGO

Here are some buzzwords you will need to know:

- *Media buy*. When you actually buy space in a media outlet.

- *Impressions*. The number of people that will be exposed to your ad.

- *Demographic*. The description of the people who will be exposed to your ad in any given media outlet.

- *Media kit*. The information pulled together by an advertising outlet that tells you what you need to know to make a decision to buy an ad. This usually is in a folder and includes demographic information, circulation information, an editorial calendar, and perhaps a sample of the magazine if it is a print medium or a demo CD for radio and television.

- *Editorial calendar*. This is the schedule of articles that a magazine plans to run in any given issue. The editorial calendar is usually mapped out several months in advance so that advertisers can run ads in the issues where the articles planned relate to their business.

to see or hear your message. If you are starting a gift business that appeals to the senior set, you probably aren't going to get your website in the eyes of the right group if you advertise in *Snowboarding* magazine.

Finding outlets you can afford that reach your target audience can be a trick. But be proactive about it—don't just let these outlets come to you. Everything then sounds appropriate because salespeople are good at putting the right twist on their particular publication or station.

Of course, with an online business you should definitely be thinking about advertising on other websites. Trading ads among related sites is a very common practice in the internet world. You can either provide each other a link to the other's website or place a "banner ad," which is a mini-business-card-sized ad that shows up on other websites' homepages. If you do these trades, it is obviously best to look for complementary sites to advertise with, not competitors. Also, try to set up links and banner ads as "windows," which means by clicking on them, you aren't drawing visitors completely away from your site—when they close the window of the ad, they come back to the page they were at on your site when they clicked on the ad.

Press Releases

Press releases are short, informational pieces sent to places that might carry the information. When writing press releases, there is a very specific format you need to follow. Press releases are expected to announce information, such as the formation of your business, expansion of your business, hiring of key employees, and awards and other recognition.

Format

Start with a title at the top telling what information will be imparted in the press release: "John Doe Launches First-Ever Internet Toy Tractor Gift Business" or "Jane Doe Receives Prestigious James Beard Award for Innovative Kitchen Appliance Gift Website."

Then you need to write a creative, snappy, to-the-point press release telling the key details of your headline. Keep press releases to just a few paragraphs. Keep boilerplate information on hand that you insert into the end of

---

Figure 6.1: **PARTS OF A PRESS RELEASE**

Title

Jane Doe Receives Prestigious James Beard Award for Innovative Kitchen Appliance Gift Website

After title

FOR IMMEDIATE RELEASE   Contact: [Insert contact name]

[phone number]

[e-mail address]

CITY, STATE—

---

every press release. This tells who you are, what your site does, why it is unique and professional, and, by all means, always include your website address!

PR Mailing List

Start an e-mail contacts list that includes everyone you send press releases to. It is then so easy. You just compose your press release in the body of an e-mail, give it a great, enticing subject line, and with one click to the group listing you can send it to your entire PR list.

Frequency

You don't want to bombard your press contacts with so many press releases they just ignore them when they come through. But you do want to send them with enough frequency that you actually do get some publicity. And you don't want them to forget about you, especially when they are doing a story in your gift topic and you want them to call you to quote an expert in the field.

Hiring Marketing Writers

If you feel you cannot write a good press release or you have written several and gotten no publicity, consider hiring a copywriter to help you out. Or find

---

CLICK TIP

Any online business needs to pay attention to search engine optimization. This drives traffic to your site when potential customers are online and in the process of looking for your product using a search engine. Keep in mind that it will take several weeks after you've completed the registration process for your site to start showing up on search engines.

---

a class in writing press releases; bring some of your samples along and get a critique on what is right and what is wrong about your releases.

Search Engine Optimization

Search engine optimization (SEO) is the buzz phrase of the web age. Essentially, SEO refers to constructing your website so that when a browser searches terms related to your site's content, your site not only appears on the list that the browser gets from his search but appears as close to the beginning of the list as possible.

A whole science has evolved around search engine optimization. Search engines all have different ways of crawling out to the World Wide Web in response to your request. A site should be constructed to maximize their crawling in your favor.

CLICK TIP

To help improve your search engine optimization efforts, makes sure the descriptions of your products appear as text on your site. If they appear as part of the graphics, search engine spiders do not pick them up. Making sure they are text means that the search engine spiders will be able to find, categorize, and catalog your site's content the way you hope for them to, and in turn boost your placement and ranking when someone searches the terms related to your site.

Search engines are what web surfers use when they want to find something online. There are hundreds of search engines and web directories available to web surfers. The most popular are Google and Yahoo!, followed by MSN.com, ASK.com, AOLSearch.com, and AltaVista.com.

You need to get your website's URL listed with each of the major search engines, and then work toward optimizing your listing so it receives the best ranking and placement possible. After all, if you're in the pet owner gift business and someone enters the search phrase, "Gifts for Pet Owners" into Google, several dozen or perhaps hundreds of relevant listings will show up. A typical web surfer visits the first listing and maybe the second and third for price comparison purposes. But, most of the time, all subsequent listings are ignored. You want your website to be in those first two to three listings that show up when the web browser searches the most appropriate phrases for your business. This is why earning a top placement or ranking with each search engine is essential for driving traffic to your site.

CLICK TIP

When it comes to hiring a company to help with your business's search engine optimization, there are hundreds of choices. You want to compare prices as well as services offered. For example, does the submission service simply get your website listed with the search engines or does it take added steps to earn you excellent placement or a top ranking? Does the service evaluate your site to make sure its HTML programming and content generate the best results with the search engines? You also need to determine if the service keeps your listing up-to-date on an ongoing basis and whether updating costs extra.

Meta Tags

In addition to accepting submissions from website operators, many search engines and web directories use automated spiders or crawlers to continuously search the entire World Wide Web and gather details about new websites (and updates to existing sites) to list. How these automatic listings are

CLICK TIP

Meta tags can be easily and quickly incorporated into the HTML programming of any website. If you decide to use a turnkey website solution, it is often done on your behalf.

gathered, cataloged, and categorized is based in large part on how your website utilizes keywords and "meta tags" throughout the site.

Meta tags have three parts: 1) the title of your site, 2) a description, and 3) a list of keywords. The information you provide (by incorporating it into your site's HTML programming) is then used to categorize your site's content appropriately. In addition to the site's description, title, and a list of relevant keywords within the HTML programming of your site, you need to incorporate a text-based, one-line description of your site, which again uses keywords to describe your site's content.

The more carefully you think through your meta tags and the more comprehensive they are, the more traffic is generated to your site once it gets added to a search engine. Many free online tools exist that allow you to create meta tags and the appropriate HTML programming, and then cut-and-paste these lines of programming into your site with ease. The good news is that no programming knowledge is required!

There are a few websites that help with meta tag creation:

- ineedhits.com/free-tools/free-metatags.aspx
- scrubtheweb.com/abs/builder.html
- anybrowser.com/MetaTagGenerator.html
- yooter.com/meta.php
- funender.com/phpBB2/meta_tag_creator.php

WARNING

Avoid excessive repetition of keywords and phrases. The search engine spiders identify repetition and hold this attempt at deception against you when cataloging and listing your site.

List Your Site with the Popular Search Engines

As soon as your website is posted on the web, you want to begin the process of listing it with the search engines and web directories. One way to speed up the process is to pay each popular search engine for premium placement (covered later in this chapter).

Why list your site with the search engines? Well, the answer is simple. Most web surfers begin their search for specific content from a search engine. They enter keywords or phrases, and then they follow the first few links provided by the search engine to reach the sites that potentially interest them. If someone is looking for the product you're selling and enters a keyword that describes that product, he will be able to find you quickly and easily when your website is listed with the search engines.

CLICK TIP

As the content of your website evolves and grows, be sure to update your meta tags to reflect this additional content. Keep in mind that it could take weeks for your updates to be reflected on the individual search engines.

Search engines and web directories are like telephone books where people can look up listings based on keywords or phrases. There are literally thousands of search engines and web directories on the internet, but the majority of web surfers mainly use the most popular search engines, so it's essential that your site is represented on these sites.

The cheapest way to get your site listed with the search engines is to visit each one yourself and complete the new listing submission form. This process is free. You complete a brief questionnaire that helps the search engine find, catalog, and categorize your proposed listing. (Note that the

CLICK TIP

A comprehensive introduction to search engine marketing and search engine submissions can be found at the Search Engine Watch website (search enginewatch.com/showPage.html?page=web masters).

listing submission process is different for each search engine and web directory.) Once you've completed the process, it will be necessary to update your listing periodically in order to maintain and improve your ranking or position.

The following links can be used to submit a listing for your new website on some of the most popular search engines and web directories:

- Google—google.com/addurl
- Yahoo!—siteexplorer.search.yahoo.com/submit
- MSN Live Search—search.msn.com/docs/submit.aspx
- Ask—countrystarsonline.com/jimweaver/submit/askjeeves.htm
- AltaVista—altavista.com/addurl/default

A quicker but more expensive way to get your site listed with the popular search engines is to pay a third-party submission service such as Go Daddy.com's Traffic Blazer to handle the process on your behalf. If you choose to use one of these services, be sure you understand exactly what you're paying for and what results you can realistically expect. For example, if you pay a service $39.95 to list your site on hundreds of the major search engines, chances are it includes a listing but not a guarantee of prominent placement.

To earn a high ranking or prominent placement on a search engine takes human intervention when submitting a listing and when programming your website in order to provide exactly the information the search engines look for in the site's HTML programming and meta tags. An inexpensive automated submission process does not typically guarantee top-ranked listings.

Improving Your Site's Ranking and Position

After your site gets listed with a search engine and appears when searches are conducted, it then becomes your responsibility to keep your listing up-to-date and take whatever steps necessary to maintain and improve your listing. This is referred to as search engine optimization (SEO) because your objective is to optimize the placement or ranking of your search.

Again, you can do this yourself, but it is time consuming. You can also hire a SEO expert to handle it on your behalf, which will probably generate

---

CLICK TIP

Keywords are the name of the game when it comes to search engine marketing. The right combination of keywords generates well-qualified traffic to your site—people who are really interested in what you are selling and have high potential of converting from viewers to buyers.

---

better results faster. If you want or need to have a listing for your site appear on the search engines quickly (within hours, not weeks), seriously consider using paid search engine marketing through Yahoo!, Microsoft, and/or Google AdWords to supplement your free listings.

If you have a good budget, you can also use display advertising and website sponsorships to ensure that your message gets communicated to web surfers.

Search Engine Optimization Tools and Resources

To find a third-party company that specializes is submitting URL listings to search engines as well as search engine optimization enter the search phrases "search engine submissions" or "search engine optimization" into any search engine. You'll discover hundreds, potentially thousands, of paid services you can use, including:

- ➡ buildtraffic.com/indexnew.shtml
- ➡ engineseeker.com
- ➡ godaddy.com/gdshop/traffic_blazer/landing.asp
- ➡ iclimber.com
- ➡ networksolutions.com/online-marketing/index.jsp
- ➡ seop.com
- ➡ submitasite.com
- ➡ toprankresults.com
- ➡ trafficxs.com/platinum.htm
- ➡ worldsubmit.com
- ➡ wpromote.com/quicklist/landing

Drive Targeted Traffic to Your Site Using Search Engine Marketing

Whenever you visit one of the popular search engines and many websites, including blogs, you'll notice short, text-based ads displayed on the page that are directly relevant to what you're searching for or to the content on the site you're currently visiting. These text-based ads are paid for by advertisers using one of several services, including:

→ *Yahoo! Search Engine Marketing*—sem.smallbusiness.yahoo.com/search enginemarketing, (866) 747-7327
→ *Google AdWords*—adwords.google.com
→ *Microsoft AdCenter*—advertising.microsoft.com/search-advertising

Search engine marketing has a number of benefits to the advertiser. You can track the success of your search engine marketing campaign in real time, using online tools provided by Yahoo!, Google, and/or Microsoft when you use their services.

Your ad campaign can be expanded as you achieve success and generate a profit, or it can be modified or cancelled in minutes (not weeks or months) to address changes in your overall marketing campaign or your company's objectives.

Launch Your Search Engine Marketing Ad Campaign

Once you choose which company or companies you'd like to advertise with (Yahoo! Small Business' Search Engine Marketing, Google AdWords, or Microsoft AdCenter are the most popular), the process of launching your campaign involves a few simple steps:

1. Set up an account with the search engine marketing company you'd like to work with. This requires the use of a credit card, debit card, or PayPal account, and a deposit (which varies among the different services).
2. Create a detailed list of keywords that relates directly to the products your business sells—industry jargon, product names, your company's name, and any other keywords you deem relevant.

3. Create a text-based ad. Each ad includes a headline, a short body, and URL that links directly to your website.

4. Decide on how much you'd like to spend on your campaign each day. Part of this decision is deciding how much you're willing to pay each time someone sees your ad and clicks on it in order to reach your website. With this type of advertising, you do not pay for the number of impressions the ad receives. You only pay each time someone actually clicks on the link to visit your website. Based on the keywords you select, you'll be competing with other companies running ads with similar keywords. Using a complex formula that takes into account how much you're willing to pay per click, your ad's placement and the frequency each is displayed will be determined. The more you are willing to pay per click, especially for popular keywords, the better your ad placement will be and the more frequently it will be viewed by web surfers using those keywords to find what they're looking for. Thus, when you launch your campaign, you must set a maximum cost-per-click as well as a total daily spending limit, which can be as little as $10 per day.

5. As you create your search engine marketing campaign, you can determine who sees your ad based on geographic location.

6. Don't panic! The search engine marketing services (operated by Yahoo!, Google, and Microsoft, among others) offer a set of online tools to help you create your ad's keyword list and forecast how many impressions your ad will receive based on your ad budget.

7. Once your ad campaign is running, you can use online tools to keep tabs on the number of overall impressions, click-throughs, ad placement, ad positioning, and related costs. This tracking is done in real time, so you know instantly if your campaign is working.

Terminology

Here's a small number of advertising-related terms you'll want to know:

➡ *Click-through-rate (CTR)*. Refers to the number of clicks your website receives as a result of someone clicking on an ad divided by the total number of impressions (views) the ad received.

➡ *Cost-per-click (CPC).* A number that refers to the total cost of running the ad campaign, divided by the number of clicks to your site that you receive. The goal is for this number to be as low as possible. For example, if you pay $100 for a campaign that generates 10 hits, your CPC is $10 each. However, if that same $100 campaign generates 1,000 hits, your CPS is just $ .10 each.

➡ *Display URL.* The URL for your website that's actually displayed in your search engine marketing ad. In reality, you can have the ad link to any URL or any HTML page within your domain. If the Display URL is SampleSite.com, in reality, the link could lead a surfer to Sample Site.com/ProductInfo.htm.

➡ *Keyword.* A specific word or phrase that relates to a product, a company, or any content on your website that you're advertising or promoting.

Online Display Advertising

Online display advertising allows you to purchase ad space on other websites that might appeal to your target audience. Your ads can have text, graphics, animation, sound, and even video to convey your marketing message. Unlike traditional print ads, however, someone who sees your online display ad can simply click on the ad, be transferred to your website in seconds, and gather more information or make a purchase.

Running online display ads on popular websites costs significantly more than using short, text-based search engine marketing ads. What your ad says and the visual elements used to convey the message are equally important. Thus, in addition to spending more to display your ads, you'll probably want

---

CLICK TIP

For many startup online businesses, using search engine marketing ads, as opposed to more costly online display advertising, is a more cost-effective and efficient way to initially generate traffic to a website.

---

to hire an advertising agency or graphic artist to design the ads to ensure they look professional and are appealing.

Depending on where you want your online display ads to appear, the size requirements, and ad content specifications, how much you pay will vary dramatically. In addition to choosing appropriate websites to advertise on, you need to select the exact placement of your ad on each website's page. Online real estate has value based on the number of people who might be seeing your ad and the physical size of your display ad, which is measured in pixels.

Payment terms are typically created by the website on which you'll be advertising.

The best way to find websites to place your ads on is to put yourself in your target customer's shoes and begin surfing the web in search of sites that offer content that's appealing. Next, determine if those sites accept display advertising, and then request advertising information. Sites that accept display ads typically have a link on their homepage that says Advertise Here or Advertising Information.

CLICK TIP

One way to generate added revenue from your website is to become an affiliate for other companies and display their ads on your site. If you include ads from well-established and well-known companies on your site, it can also boost your credibility among visitors. Pick companies that complement your gift category.

While LinkShare (888-742-7389, linkshare.com) continues to be the industry leader when it comes to administering an affiliate program, the following are a few other companies that can help you run a successful affiliate program designed to build awareness of your business and generate traffic to your website:

➡ Associate Programs—associateprograms.com
➡ Click Booth—clickbooth.com

→ Commission Junction—cju.cj.com

→ Commission Soup—commissionsoup.com

There are also many other independent, third-party affiliate program agencies that can help you create and manage your program. Using any search engine, enter the search phrase "Affiliate Marketing" or "Affiliate Program."

CLICK TIP

AssociatePrograms.com offers a free tutorial on creating and managing an effective affiliate program. Point your browser to: associate programs.com/articles/188/1/Affiliate-Program-Tutorial. Additional information can be found at onlinebusiness.about.com/od/affiliateprograms/a/affiliate.htm.

Marketing in Today's World

As you can see, even for the brick-and-mortar store, marketing in today's world is quite different from 10 or 20 years ago. The growth of the internet has had a huge impact on the ease with which you can get information about your business out there to the world. But it has also made it so easy that information overload is a serious problem, so in many ways you have to work even harder to get anyone to pay attention to your press releases and other marketing info. But now as before, getting free publicity and getting your company in front of the eyes of your potential market is not only worth it but an absolute necessity.

Profile: Karen Campbell
Campbell's Scottish Terriers
(campbellscotties.com)

Karen Campbell started her gift business 12 years ago when selling online was a figment of most retailers' imaginations. Only a year into her business, she decided the company needed a website—but back then it was difficult to find anyone who could build a website that included a shopping cart. "Now," Karen laughs, "any high school kid can do it!"

She searched for a web designer at the local Chamber of Commerce fair where she found only three. One person told Karen that her business wasn't big enough, but one, a woman website designer did agree to work with her. Karen used that website for four or five years. At that point, she found she needed more functionality, so she went to someone else for a new design.

When designing the latest version of her website, Karen took a page from the brick-and-mortar retail world. "If you go into Hallmark," she explains, "you will find a bunch of items at the checkout counter in all price ranges." She replicates that on her website. She knows that she has a lot of gift sales for teachers, bosses, or neighbors. She offers items in several price ranges, including some as low as a couple bucks so that these gift givers can find something for the price they feel they can afford. And she has a "nifty gifts" button on the site to give people the push in the direction they may need to find something to order.

One of the roadblocks that Karen has discovered with her business is that she still has many customers who are reluctant to order using their credit card number online. That first Christmas, she got only two orders on the website for Christmas presents. And she was only getting four to five orders per month overall. "I'm thinking, is this really worth it?"

As customers' perceptions and experience with the internet changed, so did their reluctance to buy online. She still has a few customers who print out their order and send it in the mail with a check, but they are the exception, not the rule.

Internet gift sales still suffer from customers not being able to see or feel the items. Karen has developed a good eye for what will sell; that includes gift cards with Scottie dogs on them—something you don't have to feel in order to get a very good sense of what you are getting. Her best sellers are Christmas cards.

"My biggest problem," Karen says, "was in deciding how many of something to order. That got easier as we went along." She admits it is difficult when something comes in and sells out quickly to decide whether or not to order more. That rush of sales could be a quirk—and then you've got more inventory that sits there. Or there is the item that comes in and doesn't sell much at all. But then there's a run on it or a jump in sales. You want to buy more but the manufacturer is no longer making them.

Karen gets her inventory mostly by attending the gift trade shows. "I got to the one in Los Angeles since my oldest daughter lives in California." And the stationery show in New York each spring is a great place to scout out all those greeting cards.

Besides selling online, Karen does three retail shows a year. Here she weeds out some items she has discovered are difficult to pack and ship. "Keep in mind that people usually order more than one item. These all need to fit into the same box."

Speaking of shipping, she does lots of European sales and has learned to ship and send those in the most expedient fashion. However, she learned through experience that some places in the world do not have reliable postal systems, and there is no recourse if the customer does not get the shipment, due to pilfering. For example, she says, "I won't ship to South America or South Africa, something I learned the hard way."

She has expanded from Scottish terriers to include West Highland terriers but says that is about as far as she is comfortable expanding her niche. Other breeds would be the most logical expansion areas but "I don't know anything about other breeds," Karen says. She is comfortable knowing that a photo or drawing of a Scottie or Westie is a good representation of those breeds, and she rejects items when they are not. But she wouldn't know that about any other dog breeds.

In answer to the question of whether online gift retailers should be sure they have every duck in a row before setting up shop or whether they should just get started, Karen advises: "Just get going. You can fix things as you go along. We've had to fix things as more online features have become available. And the site I have isn't real sophisticated—it doesn't need to be."

Chapter 7

Day 6: The Merchant Details

*W*hen Karen Campbell started her online gift business, Campbell's Scotties, 12 years ago, buying online was still a new concept. These days it is as common as being able to get Chinese take-out. However, there are still some complications and considerations you must address in order to have a smooth online retail operation.

In this chapter we cover:

➡ What options are available to you for allowing customers to pay online?

➡ What are the strategies for setting up a merchant account?
➡ How can you store data and set up customer accounts?
➡ What are the sales tax considerations?
➡ What are the other details you may not think of?

Online Payment Options

When it comes to starting an online business, one of the most important considerations is how people can pay for their orders. You must decide if you'll accept major credit cards, electronic checks, PayPal, Google Checkout, or all of the above. Your goal should be to be able to accept orders quickly, easily, and securely from the largest group of people possible, which typically means being able to accept the basic cards: Visa, MasterCard, Discover, and American Express.

CLICK TIP

Merchant account fees vary, so you need to shop around for the best deal. You want to check your local banks—in fact, if you were able to get a business loan from a local bank, it may require you to have your merchant account with it. Do a Google or Yahoo@! search using the search phrase "Merchant Account." You should also contact your website hosting company because most already have partnerships with merchant account providers, which makes getting started accepting credit cards a lot easier.

To accept credit card payments, you need to acquire what's known as a "merchant account." This is done through a bank or financial institution and typically means filling out an application and paying a fee. When your merchant account is set up, you pay a per-transaction fee plus a small percentage of the total of each credit card sale to the merchant account provider. Your merchant account provider supplies the resources your website hosting company needs to process credit card orders securely and in real time online.

CLICK TIP

Your customers expect the convenience of being able to use credit cards on your site. Despite their fees, credit cards also benefit you. Research has shown that consumers are apt to spend more on purchases when using a major credit card, as opposed to writing a check or paying cash.

By depending on the e-commerce turnkey solution provider you work with, you may simply be able to pay extra fees to them to add credit card processing capabilities to your website. For example, GoDaddy.com offers merchant accounts in conjunction with its website packages for an added $59.95 application fee, a $20 monthly fee, a $.35 per transaction fee, and a 2.59 percent fee per transaction (based on the total order). Whatever fees you wind up paying to accept credit card payments must be figured in your cost of doing business. It may be necessary to forward some of these costs on to your customers by raising your prices slightly for the products you'll be selling.

People still do some online business by printing out order forms and either mailing them with a check or faxing them with a credit card number.

CLICK TIP

Because you're operating an online business, not a traditional retail business, you need to address the fact that you won't be getting customers' actual signatures nor even swiping cards to complete the transaction. Theoretically, this increases the possibility of fraud, which means you'll probably wind up paying higher rates to accept credit card transactions than would a traditional retail business. When you apply for a credit card merchant account, you need a Mail Order/Telephone Order (MOTO) or Card Not Present account. To process your credit/debit card orders, you'll ultimately need a merchant account and a virtual terminal or gateway (provided or set up by the merchant account provider). The virtual terminal/gateway connects your website to the credit card processing company so your transactions can be approved and completed in real time online.

Still, to be competitive selling products in cyberspace, it's absolutely essential that your business accept credit and debit card payments online. Being able to accept electronic checks is also an added service you might extend to your customers.

Karen of Campbell's Scotties also warns to set your site up so that customers cannot submit orders without payment. If they don't want to pay online, they can do the mail or fax thing with their payment, but they can't just submit an order and say they'll pay later. You don't need to clog up your system with orders that may not get paid for.

CLICK TIP

Most merchant account providers can set you up with the capacity to accept Visa, MasterCard, Discover, and American Express payments, as well as debit card and electronic check payments. The fees, however, may be different for each credit card or payment type. For example, depending on the merchant account provider, you may wind up paying a higher per-transaction fee and/or discount rate for an order paid using an American Express card or an electronic check. You can try to sway your customers to choose a payment option with a cheaper rate, but the goal is to make it easy for anyone who wants to order from you to be able to do so.

The following are five strategies for obtaining a merchant account:

1. *Compare prices carefully.* Watch for hidden and recurring fees. Most merchant account providers charge a percentage of each sale (called the discount rate) in addition to a fixed per-transaction fee. Additional fees you want to compare are the application fees for setting up the account and any recurring monthly fee you're required to pay in order to maintain the account and be able to accept credit card payments. You may be offered a lower discount rate by one provider but a higher per-transaction fee or a higher than average recurring monthly fee. Other potential fees to watch out for are associated with having to purchase or lease credit card processing equipment and/or software.

2. *For a startup company with no sales track record, negotiating for lower rates from a merchant account provider is a challenge.* However, once you develop a relationship with your merchant account provider and demonstrate a track record of growing monthly sales, go back and try to negotiate a lower per-transaction fee and/or discount rate. Even a small reduction to your discount rate saves you a fortune over time and instantly increases your profit margin on whatever you're selling. You won't even have to lower your sale price, unless you want to, because customers are already accustomed to the price you are charging and will not have a clue about the lowering of your credit card transaction fees.

3. *The contract you're required to sign with your merchant account provider is usually a complex and confusing legal document.* Before signing it, understand exactly what you're agreeing to in terms of the fees and the duration of the contract. If you sign a two-year agreement, for example, but your business only remains open for six months, you're still required to pay the minimum monthly fees for the duration of the contracted agreement (or pay a hefty cancellation fee).

4. *Make sure the merchant account provider you choose offers the tools and resources necessary to seamlessly integrate credit card processing into your website (through your website hosting service).* A lack of compatibility causes tremendous headaches and costs you extra getting everything to work properly. Ease of implementation as well as security are important factors to consider.

5. *Not all merchant account providers are alike.* In addition to charging different fees, each offers its own level of customer service and technical support.

WARNING

Unlike in a brick-and-mortar store where you are presented with a physical credit card that you swipe and get a signature from the customer, online sales using "Card Not Present" accounts do not give the merchant protection against fraudulent transactions. Your sale is not protected nor do you get reimbursed for any fees.

You need to know how quickly transactions are processed and when the money from incoming credit card sales gets automatically deposited in your company's bank account. How long this takes (between a few hours and several days) varies among merchant account providers. Many providers also offer lower rates and fees to low-risk businesses. Operating an escort business, online poker site, or credit restoration business, for example, is regarded as high-risk.

PayPal (800-514-4920, paypal.com) or Google Checkout (checkout .google.com) are online payment options that are popular and easy for online business operators to register for. PayPal, for example, boasts more than 150 million members worldwide and allows website operators to add an express checkout feature onto their sites, which can speed up the process of placing an order for your customers. PayPal and Checkout allow registered members to pay for their purchases using a major credit card, debit card, or electronic check. Customers who have a PayPal or Google Checkout account can choose these options to make their purchases—their account with PayPal or Google Checkout is attached to a credit card which means they never have to give their credit card number to your site. They put their trust in PayPal or Google Checkout, not individual websites. However, only accepting these forms of payment, not major credit cards, restricts your potential customer base to those web savvy shoppers who are members of the PayPal or Google Checkout services.

Security Considerations

Perhaps the biggest concern for consumers shopping online is the possibility of credit card fraud and identity theft. If a consumer visits your website and doesn't feel safe making a purchase, he'll wind up shopping elsewhere. You need your website designer to keep this in mind at all times.

How you design your website and position your company contributes to its perceived credibility among people visiting your website for the first time. However, when it comes right down to it, in addition to showcasing yourself as a reliable, trustworthy, and legitimate business, you also need to actually put proper online security measures in place to protect your business as well as your customers.

Your website hosting service, e-commerce turnkey solution provider, and/or your credit card merchant account provider can assist you in incorporating adequate online security measures onto your website to prevent credit card fraud and other security-related problems. Although you can cut corners and eliminate some of these security precautions, doing so opens you up to legal problems and decreases your credibility among potential customers.

For an e-commerce website to be considered safe and secure, it needs to offer secure transactions using the secure electronic transaction protocol (SET), the secure sockets layer (SSL) protocol, or another form of encryption and online security that allows you (the online merchant) to accept and process credit card information and personal data from your clients without that data being compromised or inadvertently made available to the general public or hackers. Assuming you're using a turnkey solution to host your website, chances are that all of the necessary security is either already built in or available at an additional fee.

VeriSign is the leading source for secure sockets layer (SSL) certificate authority, which enables secure e-commerce and communications for websites, intranets, and extranets. The company secures more than 500,000 web servers worldwide with strong encryption and rigorous authentication.

According to VeriSign, "Without SSL encryption, packets of information travel through networks in full view. Imagine sending mail through the postal system in a clear envelope. Anyone with access to it can see the data. If it looks valuable, they might take it or change it. Without third-party verification, how do you know a website is really a business you trust? Imagine receiving

CLICK TIP

To learn more about online security relating to credit card transactions, call (866) 893-6565, or visit the VeriSign website (verisign.com/ssl/ssl-information-center/index.html). You can also come at it from the other direction and look at bank websites to see what they are advising their customers to watch for when buying online.

an envelope with no return address and a form asking for your bank account number. An SSL certificate helps website visitors protect sensitive information and get a better idea of who they are trusting with it."

As an online merchant, SSL helps you deliver a secure and convenient way for customers to interact with you over the internet. The company reports that, "VeriSign is the SSL Certificate provider of choice for over 93 percent of the Fortune 500 and the world's 40 largest banks." As an online merchant, by displaying the VeriSign Secured Seal on your site (near the online order form or shopping cart), your customers will recognize the most trusted security mark on the internet. It also signals to them that if you are conscientious about ensuring their information's security in this regard, you probably are taking good care of your customers in all aspects of your business transaction with them.

The Customer Account

Should you have customers establish an account and create user names and passwords in order to be able to quickly order from you the next time? Lots of customers like this—they can order quickly and easily without having to re-key their information every time. They choose a credit card to use for your company, just input a couple of words, and are ready to order.

Other customers avoid this like the plague! They are the ones that are comfortable ordering online but do not want their personal information stored anywhere. You need to decide what is best for your business and understand the customer profile of your typical customers. If what you sell appeals to either conservative or elderly customers, chances are they are not comfortable having you record and store their information.

Lots of times having customers create accounts is not necessary for your business. You can save yourself some headaches and the potential for lost customers if you don't require it.

Whatever you decide to do, be sure to capture customer information for your marketing database. This doesn't need to be automatic, but the name, address, and e-mail address for every order that goes out the door should have been entered into your database. Of course, you can't send e-mail marketing without first getting permission or it will be illegal spamming, but getting permission is as simple as sending an e-mail to ask. The other thing you can do is have a box on your order form that customers check if they are interested in getting information from you about special offers, on general information.

Your Responsibilities

When customers order from your online store, you need to react as if they had arrived at your brick-and-mortar store checkout counter. You need to

- → process the order,
- → accept and process a return or exchange,
- → cancel an order, or
- → give refunds.

Just because it is online doesn't mean your process is fully automated. The order has to get to the warehouse (which, depending on the size of your business may happen automatically), and someone has to look at the order and pick, pack, and ship the order. But because you are representing yourself as a business, you are required to respond to customer orders, particularly after you have processed their payment, in a timely fashion.

Sales Tax

Sales tax on the internet has become a complicated issue that surely isn't resolved yet. Right now a business that does not have a physical space in a state does not need to collect state taxes, but that may be changing. Some

---

CLICK TIP

Starting on online business is a great way to be able to work from home. A home business can help solve problems of child care or simply save commuting money and time. To truly be an at-home business, you need to keep tabs on how large your business can get and still remain at your home.

WARNING

When you take an order and process the customer's payment, you are legally required to get that order out the door or alert the customer of a back order status in a timely fashion. You can't just offer products, take people's money, and then ship things when you feel like it.

think it is unfair that those with a credit card and internet access can obtain merchandise tax exempt while those who walk into a store and use cash are subject to taxes. You should always keep up on tax law and have a tax accountant who is doing that as well.

Tracking

You want to be able to track the number of hits you get to your website. Some tracking technology also allows you to track through to sales conversion. This information allows you to know what format on your site gives you the best results. Then you can do more of that. Tracking performance is key in helping you to create the best website and capture the most sales.

You can hire companies to do this for you. Search "data tracking technology" online and see what works best for you. How much you want to spend on this technology depends on what your retail site's overall sales potential could be.

CLICK TIP

While it isn't necessary to start a business only in a category you are truly passionate about, it does help. Starting a business of any kind, including an online business, is hard work so working in something you really like can help the hard work become work you simply enjoy. And your business benefits from your being knowledgeable about the field.

Chapter 8

Day 7: Online Customer Service

*H*ere you are at Day 7. Your online gift business is set up. You're receiving and shipping orders. One huge ongoing issue is the need to constantly address customer service. Unlike some other business startup phases, customer service doesn't end with startup—in fact, in many ways it is just beginning. But customer service is definitely an ongoing element of any business.

In this chapter, you will find out:

- ➡ What are the differences between customer service for an online business and a brick-and-mortar store?
- ➡ How do you make sure all your staff is on board with your customer service policies?
- ➡ How do you use research on other online gift businesses customer service to your advantage?
- ➡ How do you establish your customer service policies?
- ➡ What are customer service enhancements and turn-offs?
- ➡ What are the best ways of handling complaints, perhaps the most common customer service issue?

Although there are fundamental customer service considerations that are common to all businesses, only you can determine what customer service means for your business. You may have outlined some fundamentals in your business plan. If not, and even if so, writing a customer service manual is a good thing. It gives you guidelines you can refer to so you are consistent with your policy at all times. And writing down your customer service goals helps clarify in your mind what these goals should be.

The Online Factor

A potential customer walks into a gift store. She shops around, picks up this trinket, unfolds that garment. You or another clerk in the store eventually walk up to her and ask if there is anything particular she might be looking for that you can help her find. She either says she'd like to browse around a while longer and you tell her to feel free to browse as long as she'd like and you are right at the counter if she has any questions.

Or she tells you that she is looking for a pick-me-up gift for her friend who is having a rough time in her life. You show her a few unique items that might make a perfect such gift. You begin to chat, you learn a little bit about her, tell a funny story, whatever.

Either way, you have engaged your customer. You have looked each other in the eye. You may have traded personal information about kids—perhaps she's in a bit of a hurry because she has to pick her son up at school for soccer practice. "My daughter plays soccer, too," you might say. Or the customer may offer a small piece of information about her friend's home—"She lives in a very old colonial house with open-beamed ceilings." "I love those old homes," you say, "my house was built in 1875 and has beautiful wood floors and open beams." And off you go.

Through these interactions, the customer has established a certain loyalty to you. She is more inclined to purchase her gift from you. And if you add on to that good customer service by assuring her that the sweater is exchangeable for a different color, the clock comes with a one-year warranty, or her gift recipient can call anytime with a question, you further enhance the loyalty.

You can continue that customer service by showing her the kind of lovely wrapping the gift will be wrapped in. Other customers may wander into the store and chat with you, showing that you have loyal customers who buy from you regularly, proving that you are reliable. The phone may ring and the customer gets to hear how you handle that exchange. This all adds to the customer's perception of you and your business and to her instinct to be loyal—she has come to like you and to like the way you do business. All of this can happen in 15 minutes!

There is little reason for customers to feel any kind of loyalty to your online store. They don't get the opportunity to have an initial friendly exchange with you. They don't get to listen in on your conversations with others. The onus is completely on you to figure out ways to replace these in-person opportunities on your website.

All Aboard

You need to make sure that everyone who works with and for you is on the same page when it comes to providing customer service. This is where a manual serves you well. Even if you don't have employees and you are the only one providing customer service, your manual helps you remember what you decided would be done in a certain circumstance and you can use that as a guide. And you need to regularly check in with your customers to be sure you are providing the top-notch customer service they want and expect.

Let's face it—online shoppers have a million options for purchasing gifts, including non-online options. You need to make sure the potential customers visiting your site know immediately why your business is a better place for them to shop than another business. And when they do place an order with you, you need to make sure that every step of that process of doing business with you was not only what they expected but also *exceeded* their expectations.

Competitive Research

This idea of competitive research comes up in almost everything you do as a business. In order to know how to outshine your competition, you need to know what they are doing in the first place. Hopefully you aren't just into one-up-manship but are interested in providing a high level of customer service to begin with. But from that baseline, you need to know what other gift stores are doing to gain and retain customers; you need to do that, and you need to do more!

Check out their customer service policies. Look at their FAQ pages. Budget some money to actually make some purchases from other online gift sites and see what happens. As you order and receive your purchase, think about the following:

→ *Is the ordering process simple?* Were you able to navigate the website easily? Were there things about the website that made it easier for you as a customer that you might consider incorporating into your own site?

→ *Are products on these competing sites showcased in a way that made it easy for you as a remote customer to make decisions?* If so, what kinds of things made this an easy shopping experience? How is the text written to be customer-friendly?

→ *Or as you shopped, were you wishing there was a real person you could ask a few questions of?* Did descriptions or product shots fall just shy of giving you all the information you needed to click an order?

→ *Was the checkout process quick and easy?* Did you get an opportunity to create an account so if you shop on this site again it will be even more of a snap?

→ *Did you get follow-up e-mails informing you of the status of your order?* Most online companies produce an immediate automatic e-mail confirming that your order was received. Then you get an automated e-mail, hopefully within 24 hours, telling you your order has been shipped. Are these e-mails helpful? Do they include helpful information such as your order number, when you might expect your order, and a confirmation number that would help make it easy if you had to contact the company about your order? A customer service telephone number in the e-mail is an important touch, providing that final gesture that you are more than just an order number in cyberspace.

➡ *Finally, did your order arrive within the timeframe you were told it would?* Did the order include useful information? A survey postcard with return postage? If the gift went directly to the gift recipient, were you kept apprised that it was shipped?

Rate your overall experience with each online gift business you order from in your competitive research. Keep a log or chart that gives you some information regarding their customer service. Steal ideas that you thought were especially helpful and make them work for you. Keep this chart with your business plan in case you update your business plan for future funding, such as for an expansion.

The Gift Factor

Customers who are purchasing gifts for other people require an extra layer of customer service to make them feel confident that their gift recipient is getting quality merchandise and whatever follow-up support they may need.

Simple exchange/return policies will help them feel that their gift recipient can get exactly what they want if the gift does not fit, is the wrong color, or just doesn't suit them. In the event of a gift item that may be subject to recall, the gift giver will want to know that their recipient can receive this information. Making it clear that you offer gift certificates encourages potential buyers to purchase from your site even if they are not sure they can get the right thing for their gift recipient. All of these things are unique to the gift business, where people are buying for others and not themselves. Remember, customer service isn't just what happens when people contact you with a problem—it is also what kind of upfront information you provide to potential customers to help them shop with confidence on your site.

CLICK TIP

Amazon.com's "one-click" service is a fantastic way to make loyal customers even more loyal. The most ardent brick-and-mortar bookstore fan has to admit that to be able to sit at your desk, call up a book you know you want to buy, and with one click of your mouse have it be on its way to you is quite a customer service boon. When you one-click a book, you get a notice reminding you that you can add to this order for up to 90 minutes—giving you plenty of incentive to one-click on one or two of those other books you've been meaning to pick up. Is Amazon the best way to browse books? Probably not. But to buy books you know you want, it is a customer-friendly site.

Providing Top-Notch Customer Service Online

The main difference between online and brick-and-mortar store customer service is, of course, the lack of person-to-person contact with the customer. But just because you aren't standing there shaking the customer's hand doesn't mean you don't have plenty of opportunity to provide excellent customer service.

One indirect thing you need to do is to enhance your website in ways that show the customer that he is always the foremost concern. Make shopping easy. Make sure you provide all the information the customer needs to convert from browsing to purchasing. The online juggle is having a website that gives the customer everything he needs to know to make a decision while still being simple to navigate. Photos and other graphics must download quickly on the slowest common denominator of internet servers. Product descriptions must be interesting and accurate and concise.

Not only do you need to make shopping easy, but you must also make purchasing easy. Although your shopping cart choices and your decisions about which credit cards you accept are critical in making purchases easy, how you set up your site also facilitates purchasing for the customer. If it is complicated to navigate from one section of your site to another, you lose your customer before he even gets to the point of purchasing.

No matter what you're selling or to whom you're selling, all potential or actual customers you interact with online, over the telephone, through the mail, or in-person must always feel they are important. Their satisfaction and happiness means they will buy from you and tell others about their great experience and your great products. Satisfied customers provide positive feedback and testimonials you can use, and they're more apt to provide positive word-of-mouth advertising on your behalf (an inexpensive way to generate new business). This is the key to your success, so every aspect of how you do business should somehow take into account what makes your customers happy.

Satisfied customers often become repeat customers. From an expense standpoint as a business operator, it's always less costly to generate repeat business from an existing customer than it is to find a new customer and make a sale. On the flip side, dissatisfied customers require more of your valuable time to fix or remedy the situation. They could, and do, easily generate negative word-of-mouth publicity for your company, which could quickly become detrimental and result in lost business. People who are dissatisfied with an experience they have dealing with a merchant are apt to complain to their credit card company, friends, co-workers, and anyone else who will listen.

The experience customers have exploring your website, placing their order, having their questions and concerns answered, and even having any problems they may encounter with the product you're selling fixed should be a positive one.

Here are some things to keep in mind as you speak to a customer:

- *When a customer calls with a complaint, first, apologize.* Unless the complaint is something that is a potential liability lawsuit, in which case apologizing can be construed as admitting responsibility, just say "I'm sorry." Don't get too soupy, don't elaborate, just apologize and then move on to the problem at hand.
- *Stick to the point.* Don't bring up issues with your suppliers or other problems you've had or people who are completely satisfied with your service. Talk about the customer's complaint, problem, concern—why he called you in the first place.
- *If the customer is frustrated, let him vent his frustration.* Spending too much energy trying to defuse him can just as likely lead to an argument as a solution. You don't need to spend your time arguing with customers,

and customers you do argue with are not going to come away as future customers. All they will remember is the argument and that they called you frustrated and got no satisfaction.

➡ *It is best to be able to offer a couple choices for a solution to the customer's problem.* "You can either exchange it for a color more suitable or I am happy to credit your credit card account." "I can speak with the company about getting that missing piece or you can just dismantle it, repackage it, and send it back, and we will send you a complete new one. And we will check the package to make sure all the parts are there."

➡ *As on online business, you are likely to do at least some of your customer service via e-mail.* You should have some automatic e-mail responses ready, but you also need to create some new ones. Re-read every original e-mail you write several times before hitting the send button. Look for any phrase or word that may be misinterpreted. Also, proofread your e-mail carefully. If it is a particularly important e-mail about a tense situation, have someone else proofread it, too. One missing word (take "not" for instance) can make your e-mail mean something completely opposite of what you intended.

Customer Experience Enhancements

In addition to conveying a professional and friendly attitude, some of the things you can do automatically to improve each customer's experience dealing with your company include

➡ setting your system up so that an autoresponse e-mail thanking the customer for the order goes out as soon as a new order is received. This gives customers confidence in your ordering system.

➡ sending a follow-up e-mail when an order ships, with tracking information and anticipated date of arrival. Online customers feel they are being well taken care of when they are kept apprised with an acknowledgment that their shipment has been sent.

➡ offering a special discount or moneysaving offer to repeat customers. Loyalty programs have long been used by many industries; there's no reason your business can't create one, too. Having one won't make or

CLICK TIP

As the owner of your business, don't delegate all customer interactions to your employees. Spend time with your customers. Talk with them, take their orders, field their complaints, answer their questions, and learn about how their experience with your website went. Although you need to fully train your employees about the customer service you expect, you can't rely on employees to provide you with this information. They don't have the investment in your business that you do, and a lot of the details may go unnoticed.

break your business, but when someone is deciding whether to go to you or the other gift source they found in their search, they will remember that a few more purchases with you might mean some savings.

➡ offering an incentive for current customers to provide you with referrals. Again, many industries are getting in on this idea. The incentive could be a free gift, a discount on their next purchase, or an entry in a raffle for a very exclusive prize.

➡ encouraging customers to interact with you online via e-mail, online, or chat, or by telephone.

➡ shipping all orders promptly.

➡ responding to all inquiries, problems, return requests, and other issues, within 24 hours of receiving them—sooner, if possible.

Offering the best customer service experience possible to your customers does not have to cost a fortune. It's all about maintaining the right attitude and conveying that attitude in every aspect of your business, from the direct interaction with your customers to the text displayed on your website. In fact, if done correctly, offering top-notch customer service should cost next to nothing. The long-term benefits to your business, however, are incalculable.

Customer Turn-Offs

As mentioned, there are lots of things your site can do to get in the way of a customer becoming a purchaser. Here are the main ones to consider:

→ Make sure your graphics are simple and low resolution so that your site does not take long to download. There is nothing that makes a customer hit the "back" arrow and click on the next site on the search list faster than sitting there watching a blank screen as your site is loading. People who are internet savvy enough to do their shopping online also have become programmed to be incredibly impatient.

→ Have the site set up so that it is not complicated getting from one part to another. The customer should be able to backtrack easily and shop around without having to go through complicated steps. It's like shopping in a huge department store—if you see something on the fifth floor but want to look at something else in the basement level before you decide, chances are you won't walk down six flights of stairs to the basement then back up six flights from the basement to the fifth floor, you'll just leave. If there is an escalator, you might make a different decision. And if there is a readily available elevator, you might be willing to go up and down a couple times! Always make sure your website has that easy elevator option available.

→ Provide all the information the customer needs to know to make a purchase. Text doesn't take long to download—the more description the better. Make sure the text is not confusing and that it provides useful information, not just text for text's sake. Although humor is often welcome, don't try to get too cute. Potential customers don't want to slog through lots of creative text to get what they need—they want information that helps them make a decision.

→ Never lose sight of the fact that if you are a gift site, your customers are buying your products for other people. This adds a whole dimension that is not there if they are buying for themselves. They need to know that their gift recipient can in fact exchange the gift if it is the wrong size, the wrong color, whatever. Make sure these policies are clearly stated in multiple places.

→ Use a shopping cart that saves your customer's purchases until they check out. Sometimes a knock at the door comes at the wrong time—a customer spent a lot of time on your site making decisions and then has to abandon her session to answer the door or the phone or attend to a crisis with the kids. If the customer knows that she can come back and finish her shopping excursion without starting over, the likelihood of her coming back to your site is exponentially better when she knows her choices have been saved and she doesn't have to start over.

➡ Make sure customers have plenty of choices when they get to your site. Unless you specialize in a one-of-a-kind, handmade gift offering, they will want to look at several different products. You want them to shop around within your site, not from your site to somewhere else.

Newsletters and Blogs

Part of customer service can be to provide customers with information they might need to use your product. It would be great for a gift business if you can capture the name of the person to whom the gift is being given—a newsletter offer just might do that. There are two ways of making this offer.

First, let the purchaser sign the person receiving the gift up for a trial e-newsletter. The gift giver can see this is added value to his purchase, especially if it is an item he isn't sure the receiver knows a lot about using. Second, if you are doing direct shipping to the gift recipient, insert a flyer into the package offering the recipient your e-newsletter. Then you will capture his contact information and add his to your mailing list for promotions as well as the newsletter (provided you get his OK to do that). And of course the e-newsletter itself will have promotional information in it.

And of course, whenever you can, you want to do both of these things!

Newsletters and blogs can be great marketing tools, but they also can take a lot of time. Find a way to keep your newsletter a bit contained so that you aren't spending oodles of valuable time on creating it. Blogs can be short, just revolving around one key point. And in order for your blog to be a great marketing tool, you want to keep it short anyway—that way you can have enough material for frequent blogs. The idea is not only to provide useful information but also to keep your business's name in the mind of the customer.

Newsletters

Use your newsletter to let customers know what you have done for them lately—redesigned your website to make their shopping experience easier, put a few things on sale, bought some new items, or changed a policy in their favor. Include information about products to intrigue customers to purchase. Make sure your newsletter includes contact information. And since you are operating an online gift store, it makes a lot of sense for your newsletter to be an e-newsletter.

Blogs

To create your own blog, go to one of the blogging sites such as blogspot.com or Go Daddy. They have blog templates and everything you need to set up your blog and keep it going. Decide on a schedule and stick to it. Some bloggers do a daily blog like a diary but for your purposes once or twice a week is plenty. Just be sure to stick to whatever schedule you decide on.

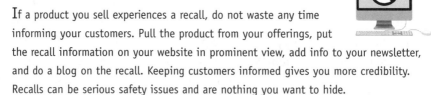

WARNING

If a product you sell experiences a recall, do not waste any time informing your customers. Pull the product from your offerings, put the recall information on your website in prominent view, add info to your newsletter, and do a blog on the recall. Keeping customers informed gives you more credibility. Recalls can be serious safety issues and are nothing you want to hide.

Testimonials

If you interact with a customer who is absolutely thrilled with a product they bought from you, if a gift recipient is over the top about the gift she received from your site, or even if she had a problem but are pleased with the way you approached and solved it, ask for a testimonial. Write down the customer's comment and e-mail it to her asking if you can have her permission to use it on your website. Ask if you can use her real name and town—or at least her first name, last initial, and town—to lend authenticity to the quote. Other customers are impressed and decisions are swayed when they can see that customers have had good enough experiences with you, your product, and your company to actually put it in writing.

CLICK TIP

Just because you are on online business doesn't mean you should keep yourself hidden from ever interacting with your customers. Perhaps there is a trade show or other public event that is key to your customer base. Attend, have a booth, let customers know there are real people out there in cyberspace.

Policies

Customers want to know what's what. And you don't want to sound like you are making up the rules as you go along. Decide what your policies are going to be and post them on your website. Returns are an especially sensitive area. Be sure to post your returns policy on your site. Don't hide it—make it one of the selection buttons along the top, side, bottom of your site or however it fits into your design.

Be fair to both the customer and to your business when you decide what that policy will be. It is especially important in a web-based business because the customer cannot pick up and feel what they are purchasing.

Also, in a web gift business, the recipient is subject to whatever the gift giver bought for them; they might like the chance to return something. You may include in your policy that second-party returns can only be for exchange, not refunds.

Other things you might want to think about establishing policies for are

- the length of time that can pass before you no longer accept a return.
- condition of the return. Can something be opened? If it is, do you discount the return amount?
- is there a restocking fee? (Common in electronics but not recommended.)
- your turnaround time for shipping.

What your policies are is up to you, but be sure that not only your customer but also any employees know them, too!

Employees

Allowing your employees to give excellent customer service can only happen when you make sure they know what your policies are and are given free rein to enforce them. Solicit employee feedback on your policies—employees are typically the ones who are hearing directly from the customers and can provide valuable insights into how your policies are being received and whether or not they are doing what you intended.

Train employees constantly about customer service. Have regular meetings, perhaps monthly, and review situations that have come up over the month. Debrief the situation and talk about the issues:

➡ *Focus on what went right.* Be sure all employees know what you do want them to do when they have to deal with unhappy customers. Don't be afraid to look at every situation as one from which everyone can learn.

➡ *What went wrong?* This is where you can talk about what caused the situation to begin with. Maybe there is a product that doesn't live up to its claims and needs to be removed from your product line. Or maybe the instructions that go with the product are missing key elements that help set up the situation for the customer to be unhappy. For instance, some types of batteries need to be charged for 24 hours before they are used to operate what they are intended to operate. If this isn't clear in the instructions, the battery will never hold a charge and the owner will be unhappy with the product.

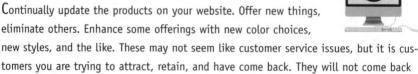

WARNING

Continually update the products on your website. Offer new things, eliminate others. Enhance some offerings with new color choices, new styles, and the like. These may not seem like customer service issues, but it is customers you are trying to attract, retain, and have come back. They will not come back to a stale website that looks like if they did place an order, the items might not be available.

CLICK TIP

In order to be able to easily and continually update your site, make sure your designer or you, if you are doing it yourself, creates a "dynamic" website. This means that information like pricing gets loaded into a separate database and when the site is downloaded, these are merged with the appropriate products and displayed. Making pricing changes and text changes is much easier this way.

➡ *How was the situation handled?* Let the employee explain the stages of what she or he did to respond to the customer's complaint and rectify the situation. Even if it is not what you would want the employee to do, let the complete explanation be given before you interject what you hoped would have happened. And then be gentle with your "correction." Use it as a training opportunity, not a time to reprimand. Presumably you and the employee have already had a private discussion about the matter.

➡ *How the customer reacted?* Did this resolve the problem satisfactorily for the customer? Will the customer be a repeat customer, or will this turn her away from your business?

➡ *Spend some time on the positive.* Besides the complaints, spend some time talking about any positive customer service experiences.

CLICK TIP

During the design phase of your site, be sure to always keep the customer in mind. One thing to focus on is continuity—for instance, does each product's information show up in the same place with the same format? Customers don't want to look around trying to figure out what is where every time they call up a new product. Look at some of the larger retail websites to get ideas about this.

➡ *Post new policies.* You need to be sure to post any new policies on your website that come as a result of reviewing customer service issues and complaints.

Keeping Customers Apprised

If customers are having an issue with an order, one way to provide excellent customer service is to make sure to keep them apprised of the status of the resolution of their problem. Perhaps you had to ship something back to the manufacturer. Or perhaps you need to replace a purchase but your manufacturer was out of stock. Have a system that reminds you to call the customers at least once a week, perhaps even more often, to provide them with a status report of where their replacement order or repaired product is and when it might get to them.

Follow Up

The last thing you want to do is think you've resolved a customer's problem without following up to be sure that is true. Once a product has been replaced, wait a few days and then call the customer and ask how things are going. This has several benefits:

➡ If things still aren't quite right, the customer has the chance to tell you without having to call herself. Her frustration with the ongoing problem will be appeased by the fact that you proactively gave her a call to check. She can now tell you about the ongoing issue without getting as annoyed as she might have if she had had to call you.

CLICK TIP

Yours may be an online business, but you still have a telephone. Pick it up and call a customer to investigate and follow up on a problem. The phone is an incredibly powerful tool even when cyberspace is your landscape.

- If things are all resolved, which is what you certainly hope is the case, the customer will already be thinking highly of your company for resolving the issue satisfactorily. With your follow-up call, the customer will be even more impressed with you and your company for continuing to care about her satisfaction.
- The follow-up call will remind the customer of your business and perhaps encourage more business from the customer in the near future.

Go the Extra Mile

In a former job, I used to hire a freelance design service on a fairly regular basis. Whenever it sent the jobs to me, it enclosed a little candy treat. I came to look forward to those packages showing up in my mailbox! It was just a small gesture and certainly wasn't something that would make me choose to hire the company or not. But I did remember it.

What kind of small gesture can you make? Considering you are a gift business, is there something you can do for the gift giver that will keep your business in his memory? Send the ordered gift from the recipient and send a little trinket to the gift giver at the same time? It doesn't have to be much to be memorable. This is one of those instances where the old cliché, "it's the thought that counts," rings true.

Handling Complaints

Handling complaints is unfortunately a good part of the customer service that you will provide. There are numerous aspects to handling complaints. All of them should be in the customer's favor. For instance, you may want to explain your point of view of the whole incident and why things are the way they are, but don't do it to the detriment of the customer's viewpoint. If, for example, you went to your favorite burger joint and got a hamburger that was undercooked and you called the waitperson over to send it back, a simple explanation might be "I'm sorry, we are so busy in the kitchen this must have gotten taken off the grill too soon. I will be back with a replacement as soon as possible." You don't want to hear the waitperson's gripe about how a bunch of people came in unannounced and Wednesday night usually isn't this busy, yadda yadda yadda. Keep it simple.

Furthermore, make up for these kinds of mistakes. The waitperson could offer the customer something complimentary from the kitchen to tide him over while he waits for his new burger. A simple gesture can mean a repeat customer with a satisfactory experience compared to a disgruntled customer who will never come back and will tell ten of his friends never to come either.

In this case too, the waitperson should be empowered with the ability to offer the complimentary appetizer without having to pass that through a chain of higher-ups. Empower your employees to deal with customer service issues. And train them well enough that they know your attitude and approach so thoroughly they know exactly what to do.

Lastly, it really doesn't pay to argue with a customer. If the customer is one you don't want to keep—someone who has proven themselves time and again to be more trouble than the few dollars a year they spend—then do what it takes to fix the problem but don't worry about being rid of them.

Every company, including your online gift business, is going to run into complaints. Being proactive and having some ground rules ahead of time about how to handle them is the key to these problems not controlling your business.

In the end, without customers you have no business. So the importance of good customer service should be infinitely clear. While you don't need to cater to every customer's every whim, you do need to be sure that customers get good service and will want to come back to your site and shop—often.

Chapter 9

After Day 7: The Tidbits
Growing Your Business, Homebased Issues, and Burnout Prevention

*Y*ou've got everything in place—a great website, an efficient warehouse, awesome product on the shelves. The orders are coming in. Your business is up and running. Things tick along like clockwork. What now?

➤ One "what now?" is expansion. Is it time to grow your business?

➤ Another "what now?" is to keep tabs on the issues of working from home.

➡ It's also time to make sure you've implemented some techniques to prevent burnout.

➡ And it's time to take a realistic look at business failure.

Let's explore each of these.

Growing the Business

Operating any business, as you learned earlier in this book, requires a detailed business plan to help you get started. Part of this plan should include a strategy for growing and expanding your business over time. Ask yourself where you'd like your business to be in, say, 3, 6, and 12 months, as well as in 1, 3, and 5 years. Then, determine what it takes to achieve those objectives and start implementing those efforts accordingly.

As your business grows and you generate more and more orders, you may want to expand the functionality of your website, add new features, and/or start selling additional products. To generate additional repeat business, you also want to find creative ways to continuously update the content on your site and give people reasons to return to your site often. Maintaining a blog or newsletter that's updated weekly, for example, gives people a reason to revisit your site (as long as the content of your newsletter or blog is interesting and seen as valuable to your readers).

Transforming a startup online business into a profitable one takes considerable time and dedication. Once this happens, however, you want take steps to grow the business. Thus, you may need to consider hiring employees, finding office space (instead of working from your home), and/or quitting your current job to operate your business full time.

To successfully transform a startup business into a profitable one also takes persistence and patience. Try to anticipate problems or obstacles you might run into, and develop plans in advance for dealing with them quickly and efficiently. If you're prepared when you hit a snag, it'll take you less time and cost less money to recover, allowing you to focus your time and efforts on more productive endeavors. Being prepared and having contingency plans in place also reduces your stress and ensures your ability to promptly and effectively deal with whatever arises.

Be sure to maintain realistic expectations for your business and its growth potential, stay on top of all of your responsibilities as a business operator (including those tasks you don't find enjoyable), and always keep up-to-date on the latest trends and technological developments in e-commerce. As your e-commerce turnkey solution offers new features and functionality, determine whether it's beneficial to incorporate these new developments, tools, or business practices into your site.

At the same time, keep up with all of the latest trends and developments in the industry that your product relates to, so you can address the ever-changing demands and needs of your customers. These trends might present the perfect opportunity for business growth or expansion—you never know when you could be ahead of the game on the latest beanie baby-like craze.

Keep close tabs on your competition. Keep track of what they're doing and take steps to do it better—whether it's providing superior customer service, lower prices, higher quality products, more attractive customer incentives, a more professional-looking website, or a more efficient shopping cart module. Try to learn from your competition's mistakes, and at the same time, try to benefit from their research, business practices, and policies, and their overall business model.

Another place to get some good information about your industry and trends is the salespeople you interact with from your suppliers. They definitely know what their other customers are doing. And they typically have a good handle on their industry overall, attending trade shows and conferences that you may not be able to attend.

WARNING

Growing a business is fraught with peril. Businesses can grow too fast and be unable to accommodate the new business. In the gift business, more orders means more product, which means more warehousing needs. Expanding businesses need more employees; employees are a very expensive part of doing business. Proceed with caution.

CLICK TIP

Start your online gift business with some idea of whether or not your intention is to grow, and if so, what kind of timeline that growth might fall into. Planning is the key to business growth being a success.

One way to grow a business is to add more products. Or you can add a few products in a higher price bracket. If your gift business has a natural niche, you can expand into other logical niches—for instance, if you sell model cars you might consider a line of model airplanes or model boats.

Buying another business is a quick way to expand exponentially. However, you need to do some careful research and number crunching to determine if this is a good way for you to go. Buying a business and merging it into your existing one can easily create a business that is bigger than you are prepared for. That is definitely a recipe for disaster. Whatever you do, expand your business with caution and lots of research.

Finally, keep in mind that not all businesses need to grow. Or they can grow in small increments—you don't have to go from 0 to 60 all in one leap. What is right for another business may not be right for yours. Just because you surf the web looking at other online gift businesses (and you should be surfing all the time) and see that several have grown doesn't mean you need to grow, too. Look back at your business plan regularly and remind yourself what you had planned when you started. Are you on the right timeline for growth per your business plan? Do you have the resources you need to grow?

Once you decide growth and perhaps acquisition is something you are ready for, don't keep your plans a secret. Tell strategic people—salespeople, colleagues, business brokers—that you are looking so they can start looking for you.

Homebased Business Concerns

A vast majority of startup online businesses are run from the owner's home. There are lots of issues surrounding homebased businesses. One ongoing issue is what happens as your business takes off and really starts to grow? Is being in your home still a viable option?

A huge consideration is whether or not you are storing your inventory in your home as well as running the sales side of the business. You may have started out with a business whose inventory was easily organized in the spare bedroom. But as you grow and increase your amount of inventory, the bedroom storage may not cut it any longer. Or maybe you can still manage to store it there but packing and shipping has become frustrating and cumbersome.

Adding to the inventory storage problem is the fact that as your business grows, you will be getting more and more deliveries. You will have determined early in the process the zoning regulations for your home business, but is your home zoned for that kind of traffic? Or is it fair to the neighbors to have delivery trucks coming and going several times a day every day? The last thing you want with a home business is to frustrate your neighbors. They have a right to protect their property values, and you want them as your ally not your enemy.

And speaking of annoying people with your homebased business, is your family going to be able to cope with a growing business in their home? Homebased businesses have a huge impact on everyone living in the home. It helps if other family members are involved—they can more easily understand the business and its needs and be more sympathetic to how it impacts their home life. But home life can only take so much impact from a business. You should plan ahead for the tipping point when the business is too much for your home and take action before it creates problems for anyone, including yourself.

Think about it—if your business is in your home, you are never away from it. The only time you can get away from your business is to go away from your home. It helps if your venture is in a separate area of the house, perhaps a mother-in-law apartment or space above the garage has been converted for your business. This allows you to shut the door and remove yourself from the business.

Don't be duped into thinking that just because your business is online you don't have to worry about professionalism as much. Sure, your customers are mostly going to deal with you via cyberspace. But you may still be on the phone placing inventory orders, sorting out shipping problems, talking with your tax accountant. Is the dog going to be barking in the background? Are

WARNING

Starting up an online gift business at home is a very logical thing. Online businesses are the perfect businesses to be homebased. However, things can get out of hand very quickly unless you plan. Think ahead about the real impact your business will have on your home. And outline trigger points that will tell you when you need to think about moving to a different space.

the kids tugging at your pajama bottoms begging for milk and cookies while you are trying to negotiate the best price on a huge shipment of widgets? These are the kinds of things that homebased businesses all have to consider and coordinate. Child care, doggie daycare, and many other services exist to help deal with these distractions that make your business seem less professional than you want it to be.

Make sure the business has a separate phone line, no matter how small you start out. This prevents you from answering your home phone and finding it is a business-related call. Even if home and business are under the same roof, there are ways to keep them somewhat separate.

The Brick-and-Mortar Option

This might be a good time to bring up the idea of having a brick-and-mortar retail operation in conjunction with your website. Sometimes this is the chicken, sometimes the egg—that is, some people open up a website as an adjunct to their storefront retail business. Other people start a storefront after they have a successful online venture. The latter is less common than the former. But starting up a gift store online as an additional source of revenue for the physical retail site is extremely common.

How It Works

Many retail ventures that were up and running when the internet was in its infancy came to embrace the technology as it expanded and matured. This was a great way to expand their own reach without opening branches in the same or neighboring towns, without franchising or functioning like a chain store. And a website did tend to expand their business, not take away from business they were already getting via foot traffic.

The Early Days

In these early days, the websites that stores created were often more informational and marketing tools than actual sales tools. They provided potential customers with practical store information like directions, open hours, and contact information. They showed what kind of supplies the store had in stock. And they often included articles and other informational material to help customers use the products they bought at the store. But the early sites did not include the ability to purchase products via the website. This was not only too complicated in those early days but customer resistance to ponying up credit card numbers and other personal information on the internet was very high.

The Change

Once technology caught up with reality and the concepts of encryption and website security were both developed and marketed enough to capture the attention of the general consumer, online selling became more feasible. Customers began to get a grasp of the advantages of online purchasing.

Customer Appreciation

Purchasing online began to be recognized as a major convenience, especially for those items that did not require fitting or have any tactile needs. Commodities such as computer supplies, drugstore items that you buy by brand, and other regularly purchased items became easy to buy over the internet. And as consumers began to purchase these items, their resistance to online purchasing overall began to fade.

Anything Goes

Today, anything goes when it comes to purchasing via the internet. With consumer confidence in making purchases online ever increasing, people are now willing to buy almost anything from a website—products, services, medication, you name it, it is bought and sold online. The staggering increase in the cost of fuel made shopping without getting in the car even more appealing.

The Added Advantage

With this new attitude about online shopping, the idea of a storefront business having a website component is almost a no-brainer. You can literally have your cake and eat it too—a local storefront with local customers and person-to-person contact as well as a business that spans quite literally the world. What more could a business ask for?

The Down Sides

Despite this rosy picture, there are, believe it or not, downsides to having a website with your brick-and-mortar store. The main downside is that you need to be totally realistic about the additional workload a website represents. Do not plan to simply add this to your already taxed workload. Increased sales means increased inventory needs. Inventory needs to be identified and ordered and warehouse shelves stocked. There needs to be people to pick and pack the additional orders. Customer service demands increase exponentially. A website needs to be kept up-to-date and fresh. The list is long—with these additional sales come additional demands.

CLICK TIP

Depending on the gift line you have chosen, consider having an open house once or twice a year so that local people can shop from your shelves. If your warehouse is too small for shopping, you could decorate your home with various lines of gifts. Serve cookies, hot cider, lemonade, or whatever. This can be a great way to endear yourself to your neighbors. They will look forward to it, and it will help them tolerate other less-appealing aspects of you having a business in their backyard.

Business Owner Burnout

One big factor contributing to business failure is owner burnout. You start out on fire, ready to conquer the world with your new business. The energy is there, you've been thinking about this forever, and now you are finally making your dream come true.

In the beginning there are so many things to do, you hardly know which thing to tackle next—website design, inventory building, warehouse coordination. It's all exciting and fresh and new, and needs attention all at once.

This will go on for at least the first year. Things are still getting organized. Now that you have set up a business, you are learning how to run one. You put in the 80-hour weeks. You can't afford employees right now and besides, in this startup phase you don't even know what you are doing let alone what to tell someone else to do. So you do it all, from website updating to picking, packing, and shipping orders, going to trade shows, ordering new product, and responding to customers.

You can't do it all forever. The best thing you can do for your business is to start with a plan on how you can run the business without it taking over your entire life. No one can sustain 80-hour work weeks for very long. Your brain turns to mush. To run a new business, to be creative, and to move your business to new levels, you need your brain to be sharp not mushy. This doesn't matter whether you are an online gift business or a brick-and-mortar retail store or a service business. It is you, the business owner, who brings the creativity and

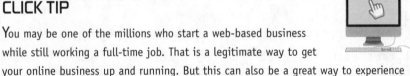

CLICK TIP

You may be one of the millions who start a web-based business while still working a full-time job. That is a legitimate way to get your online business up and running. But this can also be a great way to experience burnout pretty quickly. If you decide to leave your job and turn to your web business full time, be sure to carefully analyze whether you are already feeling burned out from balancing the two. That would be a difficult mindset in which to turn full time to your startup.

vision to the business. Nothing good comes of your getting burned out. You need to know how to set yourself up to avoid that.

It can be unhealthy mentally and physically to have your entire life revolve around your work. You may find it fascinating and rewarding, but you need to be sure you mix things up a little. This is especially true if you have a spouse and/or children or if you are doing the business with your spouse. You can both get burned out and frustrated with each other and your entire work life if you don't get out and have a little fun, too.

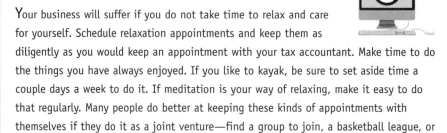

WARNING

Your business will suffer if you do not take time to relax and care for yourself. Schedule relaxation appointments and keep them as diligently as you would keep an appointment with your tax accountant. Make time to do the things you have always enjoyed. If you like to kayak, be sure to set aside time a couple days a week to do it. If meditation is your way of relaxing, make it easy to do that regularly. Many people do better at keeping these kinds of appointments with themselves if they do it as a joint venture—find a group to join, a basketball league, or at least make plans with a friend to walk, bicycle, or go to a movie at a specific time each week.

Business Failure

It can't go without saying—a large percentage of businesses, particularly retail businesses, fail within the first couple years. As mentioned already, owner burnout is one big cause. There are many others.

In the brick-and-mortar retail world, it can just be too difficult financially to support the lease of a good space on the amount of product turnaround possible. For the online business, waning interest can take a toll. You aren't paying a lease on space and you don't have a sign on the door saying when you will be open, so the incentive to attend to business is all self-directed. Perhaps orders are waiting, but they can be taken care of at any time. You can get a false sense that just because there aren't people at the door wondering why you aren't open even though your sign says you should be, you can take care of business any time without a negative impact. Not true.

The first and foremost cause of most business failures for almost any kind of business is undercapitalization, especially at the startup phase. If you don't prepare to open your doors with enough money in the bank to keep you afloat until your sales can keep the business afloat, your business will fail. You will start to not be able to get credit from your suppliers. You will fall behind on your lease payments. These and other worse financial scenarios are surefire business killers. And it has happened many times.

Poor planning is another significant cause of business failure. Your business plan is what will take care of this. Carefully construct a document that you believe in and feels right to you and you can take this business failure cause off the list of potentials.

Being overconfident is another cause of business failure. If you have created several successful businesses or been extremely successful in your career in general, you just might feel like you can't go wrong. Think again. Every startup business needs to consider the worst-case scenario.

Go into your business organized and feeling good about it. If something negative is nagging at you in the back of your mind, don't ignore it. Fix it. Here are some examples:

➡ *Overspending*. Does that web designer estimate leave you concerned about if you can afford it? If any money issue nags at you, it is probably a good idea to really assess whether you should enter into the contract. Consult the financial section of your business plan and look at where the numbers fit—or don't.

➡ *Wrong category*. Have you decided to start an online business in a gift product line that doesn't really interest you? Are you wondering if there is any way you can remain committed to this

CLICK TIP

If your business does fail, consider pulling together a team to do a "post mortem." This review of what went right and what went wrong can be the key to your next business being a success. And be assured, if you started one business there is a high likelihood you will start another!

business after the excitement of the initial startup phase? This is a major red flag—waning interest in your business leads to failure unless you have upfront plans to sell it to someone who is interested *before* you lose interest. If you wait until you have already lost interest, there is a great risk you will do damage to the business.

➡ *Business failure smarts.* Have you already had a business that failed? Do you see yourself repeating a mistake? If so, stop now! You make think things are different this time—the idea is different, the timing is different—but one of the things you can almost always count on is that if an idea or method failed once, it will probably fail again.

➡ *Pulling the plug.* It is difficult to admit when a business has failed and it is time to shut down. If you see several red flags and see things getting deeper and deeper into the negative, it may well be time to call it quits.

Despite what you may think, business failure isn't all bad. Most highly successful businesses have an owner behind them who can tell you about a few failures—inventors of things we use almost every day had rocky starts, authors of books constantly on the bestseller list tell stories of their early rejections. The tragedy is if you don't learn from those failures. Making mistakes can be the best learning experience and lead to success in the future. To learn from failure, though, you have to not fear to fail. And most failures even have little bright spots that were actually successes. Keep those in your memory bank and refer to them in the future when you start that next venture—which you almost certainly will!

WARNING

One of the three key problems leading to business failure is failing to market your business adequately. Don't fall into this trap. While marketing is important for all businesses, it is critically important for the online business. The world wide web is a big place and your business can easily get lost on it. Make sure to let everyone you know you exist. Also, be sure to do what you need to do to obtain that all-important search engine optimization so when surfers do look for your product topic they are sure to find you.

Shutting down an online business isn't too different from shutting down a brick-and-mortar store. If you have inventory, have a blowout sale. If you announce that you are going out of business to your existing customer base, you may have people ordering items in quantity because they have "always given that apple paperweight to their kids' teachers" and they want a supply to use for the future. You do need to dismantle your website and no longer have the ability to take credit card orders so people won't be placing orders when you are no longer shipping.

Some Final Thoughts

As your business grows and thrives, there are lots of things to think about. Just because the startup phase is over doesn't mean you don't have lots of creative thinking to do. This is what will keep you going after the excitement of initiating the business has worn off.

Here are some things to think about as your business matures:

➡ *The end game.* Do you have an idea of when you might be ready to sell the business and move on to something else? Is there an employee or a family member who is a natural person to take over? Having some notion ahead of time as to when you might want to call it quits, that is, an "exit strategy," is a wise idea. It will help you develop the business with selling it in mind, which will help you get the most out of your investment.

➡ *Using professionals.* When you start out, it is often difficult to justify spending money hiring professionals to do things that you think you can do yourself. However, just because you can point and click a $50 digital camera doesn't mean you should do your own product shots. Many people think that just because they can put pen to paper and write a reasonably grammatical sentence, there is no need to hire a copywriter for their marketing text. Wrong! If you did start out modestly and were unable to hire professionals, think about it more as your business matures. You will have begun to recognize where your skills lay and where you should be putting your time and energy. And your business should be more financially able to allow you to hire professionals for those important tasks that should be done by someone with skills you don't have. They will do it better and faster, both of which will save you money in the long run.

➡ *Invest your money wisely.* Focus on the things that your business category will most benefit from. You probably don't need highly professional photography to showcase your personalized ceramic mugs. But if you are selling anything that is made with fabric or requires a model to showcase, having a professional do the photos is a good use of your money.

➡ *Brand your company.* Spend lots of time and energy and perhaps money branding your name and products. Becoming a unique brand among millions of gift websites is something worth investing in. Think Victoria's Secret or Jockey. These are brands that almost everyone recognizes. A catchy name, logos, and color are all important aspects of branding. As your business thrives, you will find branding to be key—and you need to protect your brand at all times.

➡ *Get organized.* If you find that you are not organized, hire someone who is. It takes a lot of organizational skill to keep a business running. Any business, even an online one, has lots of aspects, many unrelated to each other. Keep ahead of this because becoming disorganized can have an impact on every piece of your business and can be costly and time-consuming to correct.

➡ *Get a mentor.* Find a mentor from the beginning and keep in touch with a mentor long after the startup phase of your business. You may want to find a new mentor once your business settles in from the startup phase, but don't think just because you are now over a year in business you won't need to consult with someone. Things come up all the time.

Resources

Advertising Campaigns

Google AdWords
adwords.google.com

Google AdSense
google.com/adsense

MSN
advertising.microsoft.com/ad-programs

Quantcast Internet Ratings Service
quantcast.com
This is a free service that provides audience profiles for millions of
websites. A useful tool if you want to look up specific sites for

advertising purposes or want to list your site so that advertisers can find you.

Yahoo!
sem.smallbusiness.yahoo.com/searchenginemarketing/

Yahoo! Publisher Network
publisher.yahoo.com

Affiliate Programs

Affiliate Classroom
affiliateclassroom.com/resources/travel.php

All Affiliates
allaffiliateprograms.com/travel_27/

Associate Programs
associateprograms.com

Commission Junction
cj.com

LinkShare
linkshare.com

My Affiliate Program
myaffiliateprogram.com

The Pepperjam Network
pepperjamnetwork.com

Refer-It
refer-it.com

Miscellaneous Affiliate Programs

LinkShare
linkshare.com

My Affiliate Program
myaffiliateprogram.com

Autoresponders and E-Newsletter Services

Aweber
aweber.com

Bronto
bronto.com

Campaigner
campaigner.com

Constant Contact
constantcontact.com

Exact Target
exacttarget.com

GetResponse
getresponse.com

iContact
icontact.com

iMakeNews
imakenews.com

PGI Connect
premiereglobal.com

Blogging Platforms and Aggregators

Blog Carnival
blogcarnival.com/bc

BlogExplosion
blogexplosion.com

Blogger
blogger.com

BlogRolling
blogrolling.com

Eponym
eponym.com

LifeType
lifetype.com

Movable Type
sixapart.com/movabletype

Technorati
technorati.com

TypePad
typepad.com

WebLogs
weblogs.com

WordPress.com
wordpress.com

WordPress.org
wordpress.org

Computer Security

Acronis True Image 11 Home
acronis.com

Genie Backup Manager
genie-soft.com

Scambusters
scambusters.org

Symantec's GoBack
symantec.com

Symantec's Norton Ghost 12.0
symantec.com

Digital Certificates (SSL)

GeoTrust
geotrust.com

Network Solutions
networksolutions.com

Thawte
thawte.com

Trustwave
trustwave.com

VeriSign
verisign.com

Domain Registation and Web Hosting

Bravenet
bravenet.com
Complete web host packages and domain registration.

GoDaddy
godaddy.com
Full service web solutions: domains, web hosting, site building, and SSL certificates.

Nameboy
nameboy.com
Nickname generator and domain name registration.

NameStormers
namestormers.com
Name finding service.

NetFirms
netfirms.com
Web hosting, domain name, e-commerce, e-mail, e-marketing services and technology solutions.

Register.com
register.com
Domain registration, web hosting, and e-mail services.

Sedo.com
sedo.com
Buy and sell expired domain names.

SnapNames
snapnames.com
Buy and sell expired domain names.

File Transfer Protocol (FTP) Services

CuteFTP
cuteftp.com

Ipswitch
ipswitch.com

Internet Research

Forrester Research, Inc.
forrester.com
An independent technology and market research company.

Fuld & Co.'s Internet Intelligence Index
fuld.com
Research and consulting firm in the field of business and competitive intelligence. Has links to more than 600 intelligence-related internet sites.

Hoover's
hoovers.com
Provides valuable business intelligence including company information, business news, and more. General information can be accessed for free. Subscribers can take advantage of additional content and tools like executive bios, lead generation tools, and company histories.

KnowX
knowx.com
Free and fee-based background information about businesses, people and
    assets.

Thomas Register
thomasnet.com
Get supplier information for a variety of travel products.

Outsource Providers

All Freelance Work
allfreelancework.com

Elance
elance.com

GetAFreelancer
getafreelancer.com

Guru
guru.com

iFreelance
ifreelance.com

oDesk
odesk.com

Programming Bids
programmingbids.com

RentACoder
rentacoder.com

Publicity

The Publicity Hound
publicityhound.com

PRWeb
prweb.com

RSS Specifications
rss-specifications.com/rss-submission.htm

Search Engines

Ask
ask.com

Dogpile
dogpile.com

Google
google.com

Live Search
live.com

Search Engine Watch
searchenginewatch.com

Yahoo!
yahoo.com

SEO Tools and Resources

Google's Adwords External Keyword tool
adwords.google.com/select/KeywordToolExternal

Google Alerts
google.com/alerts

High Ranking
highrankings.com/seo-resources

KeyWord Discovery
keyworddiscovery.com

SEOBook.com's Keyword Tool
tools.seobook.com/keyword-tools/seobook

Wordtracker's free keyword suggestion tool
freekeywords.wordtracker.com

Yahoo! Search Marketing
sem.smallbusiness.yahoo.com/searchenginemarketing

Social Networking and Online Communities

Digg
digg.com

Facebook
facebook.com

FlyerTalk
flyertalk.com

Google Groups
groups.google.com

GroupSense
groupsense.net

LinkedIn
linkedin.com

MySpace
myspace.com

Propeller
propeller.com

StumbleUpon
stumbleupon.com

Twitter
twitter.com

Yahoo Groups
groups.yahoo.com

Traffic Reports and Statistics

ClickZ Stats
clickz.com/stats
Net-related stats in a readable format

comScore Media Metrix
comscore.com
Internet audience measurement service that reports on website usage

eMarketer
emarketer.com
A great news source with an e-commerce focus and lots of stats

Internet Traffic Report
internettrafficreport.com
Measures router volume at various points around the world

Web Design and Site Tools

Bold Chat
boldchat.com
Online customer interaction software.

Bravenet
bravenet.com
Free tools and widgets.

CGI Resource Index
cgi.resourceindex.com
Free CGI scripts.

Direct Marketing Association
the-dma.org/privacy/creating.shtml
Privacy policy generator.

Download.com
download.com
Allows users to download trial versions and full versions of software.

FreePolls
freepolls.com
Free poll templates and widgets.

Free Scripts
freescripts.com
Free CGI scripts.

iWebTools
iwebtool.com/backlink_checker
Backlink checker.

Microsoft Publisher
office.microsoft.com/publisher
Publishing software for designing websites, brochures, fliers, and
    newsletters.

100BestWebSites
100bestwebsites.org
Identifies 21 areas of criteria they use when selecting top sites.

osCommerce
oscommerce.com
Open source e-commerce solutions.

PC Magazine's Top 100 Web Sites
go.pcmag.com/topwebsites
Get inspiration for website design ideas.

Power Reviews
powerreviews.com
Customer reviews solutions.

Prospero Technologies
prospero.com
Social networking solutions.

Search Tools
searchtools.com
Search tools for websites.

Smart Guestbook
smartgb.com
Free guestbook.

Snipr
snipr.com
Reduces long URLs and tracks unique clicks.

Stock Photography
istockphoto.com
Royalty free photos and images.

SurveyMonkey
surveymonkey.com
Free poll templates and widgets.

TinyURL
tinyurl.com
Reduces long URLs.

Web Dev Tips
webdevtips.com/webdevtips/codegen/privacy.shtml
Privacy policy generator

Web Developer
webdeveloper.com
One-stop shopping for advice and tools for building better websites.

Associations and Organizations

American Business Women's Association
9100 Ward Parkway
PO Box 8728
Kansas City, MO 64114-0728
Phone: (800) 228-0007, Fax: (816) 361-4991
abwa.org

American Marketing Association (AMA)
311 S. Wacker Drive, Suite 5800

Chicago, IL 60606

Phone: (800) AMA-1150 or (312) 542-9000, Fax: (312) 542-9001

marketingpower.com

Direct Marketing Association

1120 Avenue of the Americas

New York, NY 10036-6700

Phone: (212) 768-7277, Fax: (212) 302-6714

the-dma.org

Merchant Risk Council

325 N. 125th St., Ste. 300

Seattle, WA 98133

Phone: (206) 364-2789, Fax: (206) 367-1115

merchantriskcouncil.org

National Mail Order Association (NMOA)

2807 Polk Street, NE

Minneapolis, MN 55418-2954

Phone: (612) 788-1673

nmoa.org

Government Agencies and Related Resources

The CAN-SPAM Act of 2003

ftc.gov/bcp/conline/pubs/buspubs/canspam.shtm

U.S. Census Bureau

census.gov

Department of Commerce

1401 Constitution Ave. NW

Washington, DC 20230

Phone: (202) 482-2000, Fax: (202) 482-5270

doc.gov

Department of Labor

200 Constitution Ave. NW, Rm. S-1004

Washington, DC 20210
Phone: (866) 487-2365 or (202) 219-6666
dol.gov

Internal Revenue Service
1111 Constitution Ave. NW
Washington, DC 20224
Phone: (202) 622-5000
irs.ustreas.gov

Library of Congress
Copyright Office
101 Independence Ave. SE
Washington, DC 20559-6000
Phone: (202) 707-3000
loc.gov/copyright

SCORE, (national office)
409 Third St. SW, 6th Floor
Washington, DC 20024
Phone: (800) 634-0245
score.org

Small Business Administration
409 Third St. SW
Washington, DC 20416
Phone: (800) 827-5722
sba.gov

U.S. Business Advisor
Division of the Small Business Administration
business.gov

U.S. Postal Service
usps.gov

General Small Business Resources

BizFilings
8025 Excelsior Drive, Suite 200
Madison, WI 53717
Phone: (800) 981-7183 or (608) 827-5300, Fax: (608) 827-5501
bizfilings.com
Information on incorporating and related services for business owners,
    including forms, advice, and tools needed.

BPlans.com
144 E 14th Ave.
Eugene, OR 97401
Phone: (541) 683-6162, Fax: (541) 683-6250
bplans.com
Free sample business plans, articles, and online tools.

Business Finance
26741 Portola Parkway, Suite 437
Foothill Ranch, CA 92610
Phone: (866) 892-9295
businessfinance.com
Thousands of business loan and capital sources.

Business Plan Center
2013 Wells Branch Pkwy #206
Austin, Texas 78728
Phone: (800) 423-1228, Fax: (512) 251-4401
businessplans.org
Sample business plans and planning guidelines for business owners.

CCH Business Owner's Toolkit
toolkit.cch.com
Provides customizable interactive forms and spreadsheets, plus other business tools and resources.

Entrepreneur.com
2445 McCabe Way, Ste. 400
Irvine, CA 92614
Phone: (949) 261-2325
entrepreneur.com
Tons of resources, guides, tips, articles, and more at this informative website
  for startup businesses and growing companies.

The Entrepreneur Institute
3592 Corporate Drive, Suite 101
Columbus, OH 43231
(614) 895-1153
tei.net
Provides resources and networking opportunities for business owners.

Find Law for Small Business
610 Opperman Drive
Eagan, MN 55123
Phone: (651) 687-7000, Fax: (800) 392-6206
smallbusiness.findlaw.com
Links to regulatory agencies, sample forms and contracts, articles on all
  aspects of business development.

The Small Business Advisor
Box 579
Great Falls, VA 22066
Phone: (703) 450 7049, Fax: (925) 226 4865
isquare.com
Lots of articles and advice for startup businesses.

Telecheck
5251 Westheimer
Houston, TX 77056
Phone: (800) TELE-CHECK
telecheck.com
Provides check-guarantee services.

Website Marketing Plan
8050 Watson Road, Suite 315
St. Louis, MO 63119
websitemarketingplan.com
Lots of informative articles, as well as sample business and marketing plans.

Franchise and Business Opportunities

The American Franchisee Association
53 West Jackson Boulevard, Suite 1157
Chicago, IL 60604
Phone: (312) 431-0545, Fax: (312) 431-1469
franchisee.org

BizBuySell
185 Berry Street, Suite 4000
San Francisco, CA 94107
Phone: (415) 284-4380, Fax: (415) 764-1622
bizbuysell.com
Useful website to find businesses for sale, as well as online tools and articles.

Franchise Direct
Phone: (888) 712-1994, (800) 719-0296
franchisedirect.com

Franchise Gator
599 W. Crossville Road
Roswell, GA 30075
Phone: (678) 748-3000
franchisegator.com

International Franchise Association
1350 New York Ave. NW, #900
Washington, DC 20005-4709
Phone: (202) 628-8000, Fax: (202) 628-0812
franchise.org

Trade Shows and Meetings

Gift Association of America
115 Rolling Hills Road
Johnstown, PA 15905
Phone: (814) 288-1348
industryadvisors.com
Trade association comprised of retail stores and wholesalers in the gift
industry.

America's Gift Show
americasgiftshow.com
Directory of wholesale gift industry and vendors.

Specialty Trade Shows
3939 Hardie Road
Coconut Grove, FL 33133-6437
Phone: (305) 663-6635, Fax: (305) 661-8118
spectrade.com

Tradeshow Week
5700 Wilshire Blvd., #120
Los Angeles, CA 90036-5804
tradeshowweek.com

Tradeshow News Network
1904 Vintage Drive
Corinth, TX 76210
Phone: (972) 504-6358 or (972) 321-3705
tsnn.com

Books

The Entrepreneur's Almanac 2008–2009, Jacquelyn Lynn (Entrepreneur Press,
2007)

Open an Online Business in 10 Days, Melissa Campanelli (Entrepreneur Press, 2007)

Start Your Own Blogging Business, J.S. McDougall (Entrepreneur Press, 2007)

Start Your Own Gift Basket Business, Cheryl Kimball (Entrepreneur Press, 2008)

The Unofficial Guide to Starting a Business Online, 2nd Edition, Jason R. Rich (Wiley Publishing, 2006)

Publications and Magazines

Gift and Decorative Accessories
Phone: (646) 746-6400
giftsanddec.com
Monthly magazine that serves retailers, manufacturers, and vendors of general gift products. Includes news, trends, and product information.

Gift Basket Review
festivities-pub.com
An online-only magazine for $39.95 per year.

Target Marketing
1500 Spring Garden Street, 12th Floor
Philadelphia, PA 19130
Phone: (215) 238-5300
targetmarketing.com

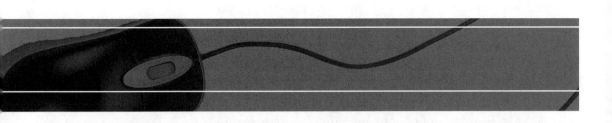

Glossary

Added value. Things that are additional value to the customer that have nothing to do with sales. For instance, including informational links on your site so customers can read more about a product or offering a blog or e-newsletter subscription.

Assets. Design elements used in website creation.

Backdrop. The area behind an item being photographed. The backdrop can be cloth, painted wood, a painted scene, etc.

Blog. The nickname for "web log." Blogs are essentially an online journal that e-tailers can use as a marketing tool.

Bookmark. A potential customer putting a quick link to your store on their computer's internet "favorites" list.

Brick-and-mortar. The slang term used for a physical retail outlet with a store-front, as opposed to an online web-based store.

Content. The combination of text, graphics, photographs, animations, audio, and other multimedia elements (also called assets) used to populate and create a website.

CTR. Click-through-rate, which represents the number of clicks to your site as opposed to simply viewing an ad.

Discount rate. The fee charged by the credit card companies with whom you have merchant accounts that is based on a percentage of the transaction.

Distributor. An authorized representative of a product manufacturer that sells large quantities of a specific product to retailers, who then sell them in much smaller quantities to consumers. As an online businessperson, you'll typically buy your inventory directly from manufacturers, distributors, importers (if the product is coming from overseas), or wholesalers.

Drill down. When customers come to your site, they will typically start at the home page. As they click to new parts of your site, it is referred to as "drilling down"—they get deeper and deeper into the site and away from the home page. If you can, your site should encourage them to go back to the home page before clicking to a new page. That way you can invite them to look at things without worrying that they are never going to get back to where they started.

Drop shipping. When your manufacturer or supplier ships their product directly to your customer, it is referred to as having the item "drop shipped." This usually saves both you and the customer shipping charges and is especially useful for large or fragile items.

Editorial calendar. Publications schedule the topics for their articles way in advance of publication. They offer this outline as an "editorial calendar" to entice advertisers to advertise in a particular issue. For instance, a magazine may be planning to have Valentine's Day-related articles in the February issue. Their editorial calendar would reflect that and encourage advertisers from businesses who sell flowers, candy, lingerie, greeting cards, and other typical Valentine's Day items to advertise in that issue.

Ergonomic. The design of something that takes into consideration the characteristics of human biomechanics to make that item comfortable to use. For instance, "ergonomic" office chairs are often equipped with changeable lumbar support and the ability to raise the seat up and down in order to fit different users and put them in a proper, stress-free position.

E-tailer. A retailer who operates online.

Executive summary. A summary in your business plan that describes your business experience and the experience of any key personnel.

FAQ. Stands for Frequently Asked Questions, a common section on an internet site that helps provide customer service by covering frequent questions.

Hit. Refers to one visitor to a website or one person viewing a specific webpage.

Hit counter. A button on a website that shows how many people have visited the site all together, known as "hits." Sometimes it pops up showing how many people have clicked on the site since your last visit. Although you want to know how many hits your site has had, hit counters on your site should be avoided as they can provide your competition with information you don't need them to have.

Keyword. A word or phrase that relates to your site's content that is a word a potential customer would use to find relevant sites.

Logo. A graphical image that establishes a visual icon to represent a company. A logo can also make use of a specific or custom-designed font or type style to spell out a company's name.

Meta tag. Specific lines of HTML programming within a website that are used to categorize a site's content appropriately in the various search engines and web directories. In addition to the site's description, title, and list of relevant keywords, you'll need to incorporate within the HTML programming of your site, a text-based, one-line description of the site (which again utilizes keywords to describe the site's content). A meta tag must be placed in a specific area of your page's overall HTML programming.

Navigating. How the user gets around your website. Navigation of your site should be simple and fast. High-resolution photographs, for example, can slow down navigation of your website and lose potential customers pretty quickly.

Niche. A narrowly defined group of people who make up a target market. The people in a niche can be defined by age, sex, income, occupation, height, weight, religion, geographic area, interests, and/or any number of other criteria depending on your site's focus.

Pop-up windows. When a user clicks on something on your site, they can be lead to yet another page or to a pop-up window. The difference is that when the user x-es out of the pop-up window, the original page is sitting there waiting. That is easier for the user and better for your site

Press room. This is the place where you can upload any press releases you produce and links to any press that you receive. Having a press room can save you time when a writer is looking for information about your company and it can ensure you are included in articles.

Pro forma. Pro forma financial statements are statements that project what the future will show. You need to show pro forma statements in your business plan.

SCORE. Service Corps of Retired Executives, a volunteer group of retired business owners who mentor startup business owners.

Search engine. The vehicle by which a query on the internet searches for keywords requested by the user.

Search engine optimization (SEO). The marketing technique that ensures that your site appears as close to the top of the list as possible when someone searches the keywords relating to your business. SEO has become almost a science and is critical to your e-tail site's success.

Secure sockets layer (SSL). The encryption of personal information, such as credit card numbers, so that it is sent across cyberspace in code rather than full view.

Shopping cart. A system that websites use to allow customers to collect products to be purchased at "checkout." Some shopping carts allow the customer to save the contents and come back later if they are not ready to place their order.

Splash page. A page of animated graphics that often opens the website with a bang. But the bang costs downloading time, so you may instead lose customers who are impatient and don't want to wait for the graphics to download.

SWOT. Analysis of strengths, weaknesses, opportunities, and threats for any new business venture, expansion, acquisition, or merger.

Template. A template in this case refers to a formatted website that offers ease of entry into the online world but also affords the developer with some customizing opportunities that can be used to make the website somewhat unique.

Testimonial. A favorable comment from a customer that you post on your website to build potential customers' confidence.

Turnkey solutions. Website templates that provide you with everything you need to get a website up and running. They are customized using a menu of colors and features that you pick from to create the look and provide the navigation that your site needs.

Turnover. The term used to describe how many times you sell a product completely and have to reorder.

Uniform resource locators. Abbreviated URL, this is basically a website address. A typical URL has three main components. The first part typically begins with www. or http://www. The second part of a URL is what you must select. The third part of a URL is its extension, typically .com (commercial). A variety of other extensions are available such as .edu (education), .org (organization, usually nonprofit), .net, gov (government), .info, .TV, .biz, .name, and .us. Sites based in foreign countries will have their country abbreviation for an extension such as .ca (Canada) or .uk (United Kingdom).

Wholesale price. The discounted price you, the merchant, pay to purchase products in quantity from a wholesaler or distributor. Once products are acquired for resale, you then mark up the price and sell them to your customers at each product's retail price. Part of your profit is calculated based on the difference between the wholesale price of a product and the price you sell the product for. All of your other business operating expenses, however, must also be taken into account.

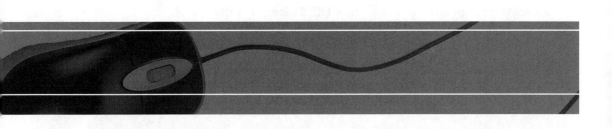

Index